ARE YOU LOOKING FOR AN
ORIGINAL NAME FOR YOUR BABY . . .
YOUR PET . . . A CHARACTER IN
YOUR LATEST NOVEL OR SHORT
STORY?

From Adoración to Izzit, Maya, Naipaul, Ena
and Apollo, the names you need are here,
organized alphabetically for quick cross-
reference. All versions of one root name are
listed as well, for a variation on an old favor-
ite, if that's your choice. Whether you're waiting for baby, giving birth to a novel, seeking a
name for your newest pet or looking for the
perfect baby shower gift, take a trip around
the world with the book that has a name for
everyone . . .

THE INTERNATIONAL BABY NAME
BOOK

BABY NAMES FROM AROUND THE WORLD

MAXINE FIELDS

POCKET BOOKS

New York   London   Toronto   Sydney   Tokyo   Singapore

An *Original* Publication of POCKET BOOKS

POCKET BOOKS, a division of Simon & Schuster Inc.
1230 Avenue of the Americas, New York, NY 10020

Copyright © 1985 by Maxine Fields
Cover art copyright © 1985 Magic Image Studio, Ltd.

ISBN: 0-671-72760-5

First Pocket Books printing December 1985

15 14 13 12 11 10 9 8 7

POCKET and colophon are registered trademarks of Simon & Schuster Inc.

Printed in the U.S.A.

To Michelle Robin

TABLE OF CONTENTS

ABBREVIATIONS

A-S	Anglo-Saxon
Arab.	Arabic
Celt.	Celtic
Czech.	Czechoslovakian
Dan.	Danish
Dut.	Dutch
Fr.	French
Ger.	German
Gk.	Greek
Heb.	Hebrew
Hung.	Hungarian
It.	Italian
L	Latin
Nord.	Nordic
OE	Old English
OFr.	Old French
OGer.	Old German
ONorse	Old Norse
Port.	Portuguese
Pol.	Polish
Russ.	Russian
Scand.	Scandinavian
Scot.	Scottish
Slav.	Slavonic
Sp.	Spanish
Swed.	Swedish
Teut.	Teutonic
Turk.	Turkish
dim.	diminutive
fem.	feminine
var.	variation

Introduction

There are flower names, jewel names, tree names, place names, biblical names, animal names, names of the months and days, names from history, mythology, literature, religion. We look for names that please us, for the most part because of their sound or meaning, or because the names are those of people who are or were special to us. The choice is great but we have not always considered wider horizons for that selection. Here are some names from various countries around the world—from Europe, Africa, Asia, the Middle East, and North and South America.

The names have been listed alphabetically, with an indication of the main language or languages in which they are used and in which they originated, and the origin, meaning or significance of the names. In many cases, the language given encompasses a very large number of countries, especially in the case of countries which were formerly colonial territories. French names, for example, may be found in many countries which were once French colonies.

Since this is not a scholarly work, the emphasis is not on the etymological study of the words, but on the best possible interpretation of its significance as a guide in choosing a name or simply to give an idea of names around the world.

The influences on the English language are numerous, varied and often ancient. It is extremely difficult to know for certain exactly what a name meant at its origin. One can make fairly accurate guesses or interpretations in many cases, from knowing the meanings of the parts of the words, but in general one cannot offer much more. Some names, of course, can clearly be translated or their derivations traced. In many languages, the names may very well be everyday words —adjectives such as beautiful (Belle) or handsome (Hassan), or animal names such as lion (Ari) or eagle (Arne)—which are easily translated. In other languages, the very effort of transliteration is difficult, since the English alphabet does not have certain sounds, and the printed word simply cannot convey the sounds of many words.

In Japanese and Chinese, with pictographic alphabets, the word which a parent chooses may have a great number of meanings, and only the written character (not what we see in transliteration) will reveal the specific meaning of a name. If this sounds complicated, the Chinese method of choosing names is so personal and individualized that in many cases, or most, if not all, only a parent will know what the name means. In addition, he has the right to choose any character, having any significance he chooses. There are no set names from which to choose, as we have in the West. A farmer, for example, may wish to call his child Little Pig; another parent may choose a character which signifies a future career for his child. A long-awaited son was born and so pleased his father's father that the boy was called Grandfather's Wish (Zu-wang). Often the name of the child's place of birth is used as part of the name, as with a girl born in Chengching (Yujun).

In contrast, in France names have been limited in choice, to a great extent in reaction to the Revolutionary idea of changing names—even the names of the days and months—doing away with saint names and using everyday words as given names (window, for example). After about ten years, that practice was abandoned and it has been forbidden to use such names. Only those names contained in official lists are acceptable. Therefore, French names are now saint names, names from Greek and Roman mythology and historical and biblical names.

There are different limitations of choice of names in some of the African tribal traditions. The Kikuyu, for example, must name the first son after the father's father, the second son after the father's grandfather, the first daughter after the father's mother, and so forth. After that, aunts, uncles and cousins may be so honored. In the Ibo tribe, a child is named after one of the four market days making up the Ibo calendar, depending on which day the child was born. He may then be given another name, depending on the particular circumstances of his or her birth or place in the family. If the child was born after the deaths of several older children, for example, he may be called Ogugua, meaning consolation, after it appears that that child will survive. If it is a son who represents the only hope for the continuation of the family, the parents may choose a name which tells that story (Obiechina—may the family live on). If it is believed that the child is the reincarnation of his grandfather, the father may name him Namdi, which means my father is still living. In the Ewe and Ashanti tribes in Ghana, as another example, names are also chosen according to the day of the week on which the child is born.

In Burma, a similar custom determines the choice of names, but each day is assigned different letters of the alphabet and only names beginning with those letters may be chosen for children born on the corresponding day. However, another Burmese tradition allows one to change one's name during his or her lifetime if desired.

Another Buddhist country where similar traditions exist is Thailand. After the birth of the child, the parents go to a priest, who chooses the name, according to the day of the week on which the child was born, as well as to what the priest himself believes to be the best choice for the particular child. Parents may also go to a fortune-teller, who will advise about the most suitable name, taking into consideration what he or she may see for the child. The name the parents have in mind might bring bad luck or be unsuitable for their child. Diamond is too hard, they may be told, for example, and so a name will then be chosen to suit a child who is too "soft" for such a "hard" name.

In some countries, even the method of childbirth can influence the choice of name. In Cuba, for example, a girl born by Caeserean section is often called Cesarina.

It has often been the custom to choose names which signify aesthetic qualities. In Japan, moral characteristics and the wish for a long life for the child often determine the choice (Kaméyo and Cho, for instance). Among Persian names, many are those of historical figures, great rulers or heroes (Bahram, e.g.). Among the Jewish people, it has been a custom to name a child after a relative who is no longer living, so that the name and the memory live on. In many cases, the name chosen is a "modern" version of the previous one or merely begins with the same letter (Martin for Moishe, for example). Formerly, the only biblical names chosen were those from the time of Abraham onward; today, that is no longer true, and Adam and others from among the several thousand found in the Bible are used. Also, in Israel today, names from the Hebrew language are also quite common. In the Philippines, Latin America and Spain, as well as in many predominantly Catholic countries, names of significance in the religion are widely used (Asunción, Annunziata). In some cultures, names are frequently used for both men and women (Lee, for example), sometimes with a change in spelling (Jean, Jeanne). In others, there is a clear distinction between male and female names and one is not used for the other, as in Thailand, for instance. In some languages, names often indicate "male" activities (Makya, eagle hunter) or "masculine" animals (Yama, bear). In some cases, we are surprised to find that names which we may think of as exclusively female are also male (Carmen) and others which we expect to be male are exclusively female

(Murimi, for example, since Kikuyu farmers are all women).

In some countries, new names have been introduced either from literature or following historical events. In Russia, for example, names have been coined in connection with the Revolution (Renat). Some of them, such as the names meaning diesel or tractor, were fashionable for a time after the Revolution but are no longer used. In France, the name of a nineteenth-century general (Kléber) is still used as a first name. There have also been some unusual, even unique, results in cases where the meanings of the words were evidently not known by the parents when they made the choices. Traviata, for example, is a beautiful opera, and the word sounds quite nice, but it means the woman who went astray. Choosing saint names from a French calendar led to the choice of Fet-Nat for a child born on July 14th, the national holiday (fête nationale) of France.

As you will see, in some cases names have versions in many languages (for example, Alexander is Sikander in India); in others there are different meanings for the same name, or at least the same name as spelled or pronounced (Ami, for example).

I hope you have as much fun looking through these pages as I had in gathering the names, learning from many sources not only what names are used in various languages, but what customs, traditions, beliefs and history have contributed to such rich and varied usage in personal names.

I would like to thank the many people I approached in researching this book for their help, for sharing their knowledge and for their enthusiasm for this project. I am most grateful to all of them. I would also like to thank my agent and my editor for their help and encouragement. Last but not least, I would like to thank Michelle for her help, enthusiasm, encouragement and patience.

I hope that the book will be useful, enlightening and

just plain fun to look through. I also hope that any omissions or variations in interpretation will not offend anyone. It is, of course, impossible to include every name in every culture. These make up only a sample of the great variety of names that exist around the world and an interpretation of their meanings.

BABY NAMES FROM AROUND THE WORLD

MALE NAMES

A

Aaron (Heb.) light, enlightened, brother of Moses
Aban (Persian) mythological figure associated with water as well as the arts
Abba (Heb.) father
Abban (Fr. from L) white
Abbas (Persian) religious martyr
Abbott (Heb.) father, abbot; var. Abel
Abda (Arab., Heb.) servant
Abdel (Arab.) used with another word, one of 99 Islamic names for God
    Abdelghani—the rich
    Abdeljabbar—the powerful
    Abdellatif—the gracious
    Abdelrahim—the merciful
Abdi (Heb.) my servant
Abdiel (Heb.) servant of God
Abdon (Heb.) servant of God
Abel (Heb.) breath, second son of Adam and Eve
Abelard (Ger.) noble and firm
    Abilard, Abalard
Abida (Heb.) God knows
Abidan (Heb.) God is judge
Abiel (Heb.) God is my father
Abijah (Heb.) God is my father
    Abisha
Abimelech (Heb.) father of the king
Abind (Heb.) source of praise

Abinoam (Heb.) source of beauty
Abir (Heb.) strong
Abiri (Heb.) strong one, my hero
Abisha (Heb.) God's gift; var. Abijah
    Abishai
Abishur (Heb.) God is strong
Abner (Heb.) source of light
    Avner
Abondance (Fr. from L) opulence
Abraham (Heb.) father of a multitude
    Abram (Dut.); Abrahao (Port.); Abran (Sp.);
    Abramo (It.); Abrami (Corsican); Abarran
    (Basque)
Abram (Heb.) exalted father; var. Abraham
Abrial (Fr.) April, name given to child born in April
Absalom (Heb.) father of peace
    Absolon, Abishalom
Acace (Fr. from Gk.) innocence
Acelin (Fr., Ger.) noble
    Ascelin
Acelot (Fr.) var. Acelin
Achalme (Fr., Ger.) helmet
Achilles (Gk.) name of river, Homeric hero
    Achille (Fr.); Achillea (It.); Achill (Ger.);
    Akil (Basque)
Achim (Heb.) the Lord will judge
    Acim
Ackley (OGer.) oak-tree meadow
Acton (OE) town near oak trees
Adahy (Cherokee Indian) in the woods
Adair (Gaelic) oak-tree ford
Adal (Ger.) var. Abelard
Adalard (Fr.) var. Abelard
Adalfieri (It. from Teut.) noble pledge
Adalia (Heb.) God is my refuge
Adalric (OGer.) noble ruler
    Adelric
Adam (Heb.) red earth, soil from which Adam was
    created

Adamo, Adan (Sp.); Adao (Port.); Adnot, Adné,
   Adanet (Fr.); Addis, Addison, MacAdam, var.
   Adamson

Adar (Heb.) noble; in Jewish calendar, name of one of
   spring months

Addison (OE) son of Adam
   Addis

Addula (Teut.) noble cheer

Addy (Teut.) awesome, noble
   Addie, Ade, Ado

Adelar (Teut.) noble eagle

Adelard (Ger.) var. Abelard
   Adal, Adalard

Adelphe (Fr. from Gk.) brother

Ademar (Fr. from Teut.) fierce, noble, famous
   Ademaro (It.)

Ader (Heb.) flock

Adham (Arab.) black

Adhar (Arab.) waiting

Adib (Arab.) man of letters

Adin (Heb.) decorative

Adir (Heb.) noble, mighty

Adita (Omaha Indian) priest

Adiv (Arab.) pleasant, gentle

Adlai (Heb.) refuge of God; (Arab., Heb.) just
   Adley

Adly (Arab.) my justice

Admon (Heb.) red peony

Adnah (Heb.) adorned
   Adin

Adnan (Turk.) heaven

Adon (Heb.) Lord

Adonijah (Heb.) God is my Lord

Adonis (Gk.) mythological figure, beautiful young man
   loved by Aphrodite

Adoram (Heb.) beauty

Adrian (L) of the Adriatic, Roman emperor
   Adrien (Fr.); Adriano (It.); Adiran (Basque);
   Hadrian

21

Adriel (Heb.) the Lord is my God
Aelig (Fr.) Breton name; (Gk.) angel, messenger
Aeneas (L) hero of epic; (Gk.) unique choice
    Angus (Irish, Scot.)
Afdal (Arab.) excellent
Afif (Arab.) virtuous
Afifi (Arab.) my chastity, honest
Agathon (Fr., Ger. from Gk.) good
Aggae (Heb.) festival of the Lord
Agnan (Fr. from L) innocent, pure
Agnolo (It.) angel
Agur (Heb.) gatherer
Ahab (Heb.) father's brother
Ahern (Celt.) lord of horses; (OE) heron
    Ahearn
Ahmad (Arab.) praiseworthy; var. Mahmoud
    Ahmed
Ahmik (Chippewa Indian) beaver
Ahsan (Arab.) charity
    Ehsan, Ihsan
Aidan (Celt.) fire; (OFr.) help
Aimé (Fr.) beloved
Aimery (Teut.) industrious ruler; also king's house;
    var. Emery, Aimeric, Aymeric (Fr.); Imre
    (Hung.)
Aimon (Fr. from Teut.) house
    Aimond, Haimon, Aymon, Héman
Ainsley (OE) Ann's meadow
    Ainslie, Ainsworth
Aiyedun (Yoruba, West Africa) life is good
Ajala (Yoruba, West Africa) potter in Yoruba poem
Akash (Hindi) sky
Akbar (Arab.) great
Akevy (Hung.) Jacob
Akiba (Heb.) Jacob
    Akub, Akiva
Akikta (Sioux Indian) works with determination
Akim (Russ.) short Jehoiakim

Akiva (Heb.) protect; var. Jacob
    Kiva, Kivi
Akmal (Arab.) perfect
Akram (Arab.) noble, generous
Alaire (Fr. from L) joyous; var. Hilary, Hilaire, Alair,
    Hélier, Lary
Alam (Arab.) universe
Alan (Gaelic) handsome, cheerful
    Allen, Allan; Alin, Alain (Fr.)
Alard (OGer.) nobly resolute
    Adlar, Allard
Alaric (Ger.) ruler of all; (L) chosen
Alastair (Scot.) Alexander
    Allister
Alaui (Arab.) high
Alawi (Arab.) follower of Ali
Alban (Fr., L) white
    Albain, Albin, Alby, Albinet, Alba, Alva
Alberic (OGer.) leader, king
    Aubrey
Albern (OGer.) noble valor
Albert (Fr. from OGer.) noble, bright
    Alberto (It., Sp.); Adelbrecht, Adalbert,
    Adelbert, Albrecht, Ulbricht (Ger.); Bert, Ailbert
Alcander (Gk.) strong
    Alcinder
Alden (OE) antiquity
    Aldo (It.); Aldous, Aldus, Aldivin, Eldon, Aldon
Aldin (OE) great friend
    Aldwin, Alden
Aldous (OGer.) wise; var. Alden, Aldin
    Aldus
Aldred (OE) great counsel
    Eldred
Aldrich (OE) wise
    Alric, Aldric
Aldwin (OE) old friend; var. Aldin
Alec—short Alexander

Alem (Arab.) wise man

Aleron (L) winged

Alex—short Alexander

Alexander (Gk.) defender of men, helper of men
Alexandre (Fr.); Alejandro (Sp.); Alessandro (It.); Sikander (Hindi); Iskander (Ethiopian); Sasha (Russ. dim.); Alessandri (Corsican); Sandro (It.); Sandor (Hung.); Alastair (Scot.); Sander, Saunder, Alix, Alex, Alec, Alick, Al

Alexis—short Alexander

Alf (Scand.) elf; short Alfred

Alfeo (It., Sp.) Alfred

Alfie—dim. Alfred

Alfonso (It.) Alphonse

Alfred (OE) wise
Alfredo (It., Sp.); Fredo, Fred, Avery, Alf, Alfie, Al

Alger (A-S) noble warrior; also short Algernon
Elgar, Elger

Algernon (OFr.) with mustache

Algis (Fr. from Teut.) spear

Ali (Arab.) noble, sublime

Alim (Arab.) scholar

Alin (Fr. from Teut.) all

Allister—var. Alexander

Almund (Teut.) protection

Alon (Heb.) oak tree

Alonso (Sp. from Teut.) eager for battle; var. Alphonso
Alonzo, Lonny

Aloys (Fr. from Teut.) wise

Aloysius (Ger.) var. Louis

Alphonse (OGer.) noble, ready
Alonso, Alphonse (Fr.); Alfonso (It.)

Alroy (L) king

Alto (Sp. from L) alto

Alton (OE) village

Alvan (L) white
Alban, Alvin, Alwin, Alwyn, Elvin, Elvis

Alvin (Ger.) beloved by all
    Alvan
Alvis (Norse) wise
Amaan (Arab.) protection
Amadeus (L) love God, loving God
    Amadeo (It.); Amado (Sp.); Amadei (Corsican);
    Amyot, Amyas, Amadieu (Fr.)
Amadour (Fr. from L) lovable
Amaël (Fr. from Celt.) prince
Amal (Arab.) hope; (Heb.) work
Amana (Heb.) faithful
Amand (Fr.) deserving of love
Amando (It.) loving
Amar (Hindi) immortal
Amaro (Port.) dark, moor
Amaubert (Fr. from Teut.) famous, bright
    Maubert
Ambar (Hindi) sky
Ambert (OGer.) bright
Ambrose (Gk.) immortal, divine
Amelek (Heb.) grandson of Esau
Amelin (Fr.) var. Amaubert
    Melin, Amelot
Amer (Arab.) full, plentiful
Amery (L) loving one
    Amory, Emory; Imre, Imray, Imrie (Hung.);
    Amerigo (It.)
Amias (L) love God; (Fr.) from Amiens
Amiel (Heb.) God of my people; (Fr.) var. Emile
Amil (Arab.) industrious
Amilcar (Sp.) Phoenician king
Amin (Arab., Heb.) trustworthy, honest
Amir (Arab.) prince; (Persian) king
Amiram (Heb.) my people is exalted
Amitai (Heb.) truth
    Amiti
Amitan (Heb.) true, faithful
Amjad (Arab.) glorious

Ammar (Arab.) builder

Ammi (Heb.) my people

Ammon—ancient Egyptian god, associated with life and reproduction

Amnon (Heb.) faithful
  Amon

Amos (Heb.) borne by God

Amoz (Heb.) strong

Amram (Arab.) life; (Heb.) mighty nation

Amyot (Fr.) beloved

Anam (Arab.) the people

Anan (Heb.) cloud

Anand (Hindi) peaceful

Anastasius (Gk.) resurrection, immortality
  Anastase (Fr.); Anastagio (It.); Anastasio (Sp.); Anastasi (Basque)

Anatole (Fr. from Gk.) from the East
  Anatol; Anatolio (It., Sp.), Anatoli (Basque); Anatoly (Russ.)

Ancelot (Fr.) var. Lancelot

Anchali (Taos Indian) painter

Ancher (OE) anchor

Anders (Scand.) Andrew

Andrew (L) manly
  André (Fr.); Andrea, Andreas (It.); Andrés (Sp.); Ander (Basque); Andrei, Andrej (Pol., Russ.); Anders, Anderson (Scand.); Andreas (Ger.); Andrin, Andreu, Andrieu, Andral (Fr. var.)

Andros (Pol.) mythological god of the seas

Angat—African mythological prince of the sea

Angeda (Omaha Indian) from every direction

Angel (Gk., Sp.) messenger
  Angelo (It.); Gotzon (Basque)

Angus (Irish, Scot.) Aeneas

Anibal (Gk.) grace of the Almighty
  Hannibal (Sp.)

Anicet (Fr., Gk.) unconquered
  Anikita (Russ.)

Anniss (Arab.) charming

Anoki (American Indian) actor
Anoush (Persian) eternal
Ansari (Arab.) helper
Ansel (Fr.) servant; var. Ancelot, Anselm
Anselm (Teut.) divine helmet
    Anselmo (Sp.); Anselme (Fr.)
Anshar (Teut.) divine spear
Anson (A-S) Ann's son
Antal (Hung. fr. L) inestimable
    Antek, Antoni (Pol.); Antolin (Ger.); Anton
    (Ger., Russ.); Antos (Port.)
Anthony (L) inestimable, beyond praise
    Antoine (Fr.); Anton (Ger., Slav.); Antonio (It.,
    Sp.); Antonin (Slav.); Antonino, Antony, Tonio,
    Tonino
Anwar (Arab.) luminous
    Anour, Anouar
Apolinario (Sp.) Apollo
Apollo (Gk.) manly
Aqiyl (Arab.) wise
Aquilino (L, Sp.) eagle
Araceli (L, Sp.) altar of heaven
Aram (Heb.) biblical name for ancient Syria; high
Aran (Thai) forest
Arash (Persian) hero
Arbie (OFr.) crossbow
Archambaud (Fr., Teut.) excellent, bold
    Archibald
Archer (L) bowman
Archibald (OGer.) genuine, bold
    Archie
Ardel (OE) from the valley
    Ardell
Arden (L) eager, fervent
    Ardin
Ardon (Heb.) bronze
Areh (Teut.) ever king
Arel (Heb.) lion of God
Arend—var. Arnold

Aretino (Gk., It.) victorious
Argus (Gk.) mythological all-seeing giant; vigilant
Ari (Teut.) eagle; (Heb.) lion
    Ario, Aryeh
Ariel (Heb.) lion of God
    Arel, Areli
Arion (Heb.) melodious
Aristedes (Gk.) son of the best
    Aristide (Fr.)
Aristo (Gk.) the best
Aristotle (Gk.) the best
Arkady (Russ.) Archibald
Arland—var. Orlando, Arlen
    Arlando
Arlen (Celt.) pledge
    Arlin, Arland
Arley (Heb.) pledge
    Arleigh, Arland, Arlin, Arlen, Arles, Arlyn, Arliss, Arlie, Arlo
Arlo (Heb.) pledge; (OE) fortified hill; var. Harlow
Arman (Persian) desire, goal
Armand (Fr., Teut.) soldier; var. Herman
    Armando (Sp.); Armanno, Armino (It.);
    Armin, Armond (Fr.)
Armel (Celt., Fr.) prince
Armon (Heb.) castle
Arnaldo (Ger., Sp.) strong
    Arnoldo
Arnaud (Fr., Ger.) strong
    Aulnay
Arne (OGer.) eagle
Arno—short Arnold
Arnold (OGer.) eagle, power
    Arnot, Arnaud, Arnoll, Arnott, Arnet, Arnett, Arnald (Fr.); Arend, Arnall (Dut.); Arnaldo, Arnoldo (Sp.); Arndt (Ger.)
Arnon (Heb.) roaring stream
Aroon (Thai) dawn

Arri (L) honorable
Arrian (Dut., L) of the Adriatic
Arrigo (It.) Harry
    Arrighetto, Alrigo
Arsen (Gk.) strong
Arsenius (L) powerful
    Arsenio (Sp.); Arsène (Fr.)
Arsha (Persian) venerable
Arthur (A-S) eaglelike; high, noble
    Artur (Fr.); Arturo (It., Sp.); Arth (Scot.); Atty
    (Irish)
Arun (Hindi) dawn; red color
Arvad (Heb.) wanderer
    Arvid, Arv
Arval (L) cultivated land
Arvid (A-S, Scand.) friend of the people
    Arvin, Arv, Arve
Asa (Heb.) healer
Asad (Arab.) lion
Asael (Heb.) God has created
    Asiel
Asaph (Heb.) gather
    Asaf
Ascelin (Fr., Teut.) noble
    Asselin
Asgard (ONorse) court of god
Ashby (Scand.) ash-tree farm
Asher (Heb.) happy, fortunate
Ashford (OE) ford near ash tree
Ashir (Arab.) happiness
Ashley (OE) ash-tree meadow
Ashlin—var. Ascelin
    Aslin, Acelet (Fr.)
Ashok (Hindi) without sadness
Ashraf (Arab.) honorable
Ashton (OE) ash-tree farm
Ashwani (Hindi) first of 27 galaxies revolving around
    the moon

Asir (Heb.) to bind
Asnee (Thai) lightning
Assefa (Ethiopian) enlarge
Asvald (Nor., Teut.) divine power
Asvard (Nor., Teut.) divine ward
Asvor (Nor., Teut.) divine prudence
Atalik (Hung.) fatherlike
    Atli (Nor.); Atilio (It.)
Ataollah (Arab.) gift of God
Atepa (Choctaw Indian) wigwam
Athan (Gk.) immortal
Athanasius (Gk.) immortality; var. Anastasius
Athos (Gk.) name for Zeus
Atiq (Arab.) old
Atli (ONorse) Attila, King of the Huns
Atwater (OE) waterside
Atwell (OE) spring, fountain
Atwood (OE) forest
Aubert (Fr.) var. Albert
    Auver, Aubé, Aubrey
Aubrey (OGer.) ruler; var. Albert
    Avery, Auberon, Oberon, Alberic
Audebert (Fr., OGer.) old, shining
    Audibert, Aldebert
Audemar (OFr.) old, famous
Audie (OGer.) noble, strong
Audon (OFr.) old, rich
    Audelon
Audren (Fr.) royal
Audry (OFr., Teut.) old, powerful
    Aldric
Augustus (L) venerable
    Austin, Augustin, August
Aurelio (L, Sp.) gold
Auric (Fr., Teut.) all powerful
    Alric, Alriq
Aurick (Ger.) protecting ruler
    Warrick

Austin—short Augustin, Augustus
Ave (L) hail
Avel (Heb., Russ.) breath
Avelin (OFr.) hazelnut
  Avenel
Avent (OFr.) name given to child born during Advent
  Aventin—saint name
Averell (OE) warrior
  Averel, Averil, Avcrill
Averil (OE) wild boar; (A-S, L) opening of earth
  for spring; var. April
Avery (A-S) ruler of elves; var. Alfred
Avi (Heb.) father
Avidan (Heb.) father of justice, God is just
Avidor (Heb.) father of a generation
Aviel (Heb.) God is my father
  Abiel
Avigdor (Heb.) father of protector
Avis (L) bird; (Ger.) refuge in battle
Avital (Heb.) father of dew
Aviv (Heb.) spring, youth
Avner (Heb.) var. Abner
Avniel (Heb.) God is my strength
Avram (Heb.) father of a mighty nation
  Abram, Abraham
Avril (Fr.) April
Awad (Arab.) reward, compensation
Axel (Heb.) father of peace; (OGer.) small oak tree;
  (L) axe
  Aksel
Ayani (Navajo Indian) buffalo
Aylmer (Ger.) awesome fame
Aylsworth (Ger.) awesome worth
Aylward (Ger.) formidable guardian
Aylwin (Ger.) awesome friend
Aymon (Fr.) var. Raymond, Haymon
Ayub (Arab.) Job, penitent
  Ayoub

Azaria (Heb.) God is my help
Azariah (Heb.) God helps
Azem (Arab.) bones
Aziz (Heb.) strong
Azriel (Heb.) God is my help

B

Babatunde (Yoruba; West Africa) father returns
Bachir (Arab.) herald, good omen
Badawz (Arab.) Bedouin
Baha (Arab.) a wonder
Bahar (Arab.) sailor
Bahram (Persian) ancient king
Bailey (OFr.) bailiff
Baird (Gaelic) poet
Baith (Arab.) he raises (one of attributes of God in Islam)
Baldassare (It.) Balthazar
Baldwin (OGer.) bold friend
Balfour (Scot.) pastureland; Lord A.J. Balfour, author of Balfour Declaration in favor of Jewish State, 1917
Ballard (OGer.) strong
Balor (OFr.) bale maker
Balraj (Hindi) strongest
Bancroft (OE) from the bean field
Barak (Heb.) flash of light, lightning
Baram (Heb.) son of the nation
Barasa (Kikuyu, Kenya) meeting place
Barclay (OE) birch meadow
    Berkely
Bard (Gaelic) poet
    Baird

Barden (OE) boar's den
Bardo (Dan.) short Bartholomew
Bardon (A-S) barley valley
Barend (Dut.) firm bear
Bari (Arab.) the maker (one of attributes of God in
    Islam)
Barker (OE) birch tree
    Birk (Scot.)
Barlow (OE) boar's hill, bare hill
Barnabas (Heb.) son of prophecy
    Barnaba (It.); Bernabé (Sp.); Barnabé (Fr.);
    Barna
Barnaby (Aramaic) speech
Barnard (Fr.) var. Bernard
Barnes (OE) bear
Barnet—var. Bernard
Barnett (OE) noble
Barney—short Bernard, Barnaby, Barnett
Baron (OE) nobleman
Barrett (Teut.) bearlike
Barris—var. Barry
Barry (Celt.) good marksman; (Welsh) son of Harry;
    (OFr.) barrier; dim. Baruch, Barnett
Bart (Heb.) short Bartholomew
Barth (Fr.) var. Bartholomew
Bartholomew (Aramaic) son of Talmai (ploughman)
    Bartley (Irish); Bartolomé (Sp.); Bartol, Bardol
    (Basque); Bartholomé, Bertélemy, Bartoli,
    Barthel, Barthol (Fr.); Bartek (Pol.); Bartel
    (Ger.); Bartlett, Bartley
Barton (OE) barley farm
Bartram (OGer.) bright raven
Baruch (Heb.) blessed
Baruilai (Heb.) man of iron
Basam (Arab.) smiling
    Basem, Basim
Basil (Gk.) kingly; (Arab.) brave
    Basilio (It., Sp.); Basilius (Ger.); Vassily (Russ.)

Basilyr (Arab.) insight
Ba Tu (Burmese) like his father
Baud (Fr. from OGer.) bold
Baxter (OE) baker
Bay (Fr.) color of horse
Bayard (Teut.) red-brown hair
Baylor (A-S) horse trainer
Beasley (OE) field of peas
Beau (Fr.) handsome; var. Baud
Beaumont (Fr.) beautiful mountain
Beauregard (Fr.) beautiful view
Beauvais (Fr.) var. Bevis
Bede (OE) prayer
Bedell (OE) messenger
Behram—Persian mythological figure
Behras (Persian) beautiful as day
Behrooz (Persian) lucky, hopeful
Behzad (Persian) noble
Bekele (Ethiopian) sprout, come into being
Bela (Slav.) white
Belden (Teut.) beautiful valley
 Beldon
Bellamy (Fr.) beautiful friend
Belton (OFr.) beautiful town
Beltran (Ger.) brilliant
Bemus (Gk.) platform
Ben (Heb.) son
Ben-Ami (Heb.) son of my people
Bénad (Fr.) var. Bernard
 Bénard
Benedict (L) blessed
 Benoit (Fr.); Benedetto (It.); Benedicto (Sp.);
 Benigno, Benito (It., Sp.); Benin (Basque)
Benjamin (Heb.) fortunate, strong (son of the right
 hand)
 Beniamino (It.); Benjamin (Sp.); Benkamin
 (Basque)
Bennett—short Benedict
Benoni (Fr., Heb.) son of sadness

Benroy (Heb.) son of lion
    Ben-Aray
Benson—short Ben Zion (Heb.) excellent son; also
    Ben's son
Bentley (OE) moor
Benton (OE) moor dweller
Berakhiah (Heb.) God blesses
Berard (Fr.) var. Bernard
Béraud (Fr. from Teut.) strong leader
    Beraut
Bérenger (Fr.) var. Bernard
    Baranger
Berhanu (Ethiopian) his light
Beriah (Heb.) creature
Berkeley (A-S) birch meadow
    Barclay
Bernard (OGer.) courage of bear
    Bernon, Bernot (Fr.)
Bert (Teut.) bright
Bertell (Swed.) bright
    Bertil, Berthold, Bertol, Bertram
Bertold (Fr., Ger.) brilliant, famous leader
    Berthaud, Berthold
Berton (Teut.) glorious raven
    Bertin
Bertram (Teut.) bright raven
Bertrand (Fr.) brilliant
    Bertran, Bertram, Beltran
Bertwin (Teut.) bright friend
Berwick (OE) barley grange
Berwin (Teut.) warrior friend
Beryl (Gk.) sea-green gem; (Heb.) precious stone,
    perhaps topaz; (Yiddish) dim. Ger. word for bear
Bes—Egyptian god of pleasure and guardian of the
    home
Bevan (Celt.) son of Evan, young warrior
Beverly (OE) bcaver meadow
Bevis (OFr.) bull; (Teut.) bowman
    Bevys

Bhagat (Arab.) joy
Bibiano (Sp.) var. Vyvyan
Bienvenido (Sp.) welcome
Bijan (Persian) ancient hero
Bildad (Heb.) beloved
Bilguy (Arab.) joy
    Bilgai
Billie—nickname William
Bion (Gk.) life
Birch (A-S) tree name, white
Bjorn (Swed.) bear
Blagdon (OE) dark valley
Blagoslav (Pol.) good glory
Blaine (OE) source of a river; (Celt.) thin
Blair (Celt.) from the plain
Blais (Fr.) stammerer; (Gk.) royal
    Blaise
Blake (OE) dark
Blakeley (OE) dark meadow
Blandon (L) gentle
Blase (Gk.) flat-footed
    Blas (Sp.); Braz (Port.); Vlass (Russ.)
Boaz (Heb.) strong, swift, Ruth's second husband in
    Bible
Bodaway (American Indian) fire maker
Boden (OFr.) herald
Bo Gale (Burmese) little officer
Bogdan (Pol.) God's gift
    Bohdan
Boliston (Gk.) earth, clay
Bolton (OE) manor farm
Bonaro (It., Sp.) friend
Bonaventure (Fr.) happy destiny
Bond (A-S) to bind, till the soil
Boniface (L) welldoer
    Bonifacio (It., Sp.); Bonifazio (It.)
Booker (A-S) beech tree
Booth (OE) hut, market stall
Borden (A-S) boar valley, cottage

Borg (ONorse) castle
    Borje
Boris (Hung.) stranger; (Russ.) fight, warrior
Borka (Russ.) fight
    Borinka—dim.
Bosley (OE) grove of trees
Boucard (Fr., Teut.) beech tree
    Bouchard, Bouchand
Boutros (Arab.) Peter
Bowden (A-S) herald
    Boyden
Bowen (Celt.) son of Owen; var. Evan
Boyce (Welsh) county in central Wales; (Fr.) woodland
Boyd (Celt.) yellow, blond
Boynton (Celt.) river in Ireland
Braden (OE) broad valley
Bradford (OE) from broad ford
Bradley (OE) from broad meadow
Bradwell (OE) from broad spring
Brady (A-S) broad island
Brage—Norse god of poetry
    Bragi
Braham (Hindi) creator
Bram (Dut.) short Abraham
Bran (Irish) raven
    Brand, Brandon, Brondon, Brennan, Brent,
    Brant, Brend
Brand (Scand.) flame, sword blade; (OFr.) sword
Brandon (OE) from lighted hill
Brant (Teut.) firebrand
Braxton (A-S) Brock's town
Bray (OE) cry out
Brendan (OGer.) flame; var. Bran; (Gaelic) little raven
Brent (OE) from steep hill
Bret (Celt.) from Brittany
Brewster (OE) brewer
Briac (Celt., Fr.) estime
Brian (ONorse) strong
    Bryan, Bryant, Brien, Brion

Briand (Fr.) castle
Brice (A-S) son of nobleman; (Celt.) estime
    Bryce, Brick
Brieg (Celt., Fr.) estime
Brigham (OE) bridge enclosure; (OFr.) troops
Brigman—var. Brigham
Brin (Fr. from Teut.) bear
Brinley (OE) tawny
Brinton—English town in Norfolk
Bristol—var. Brice
Brit (Celt.) Britain; speckled
    Briton
Broc (Fr.) badger
Brock (OE) badger
Broderick—combination Brad and Richard; (Welsh)
    son of Roderick; (Teut.) famous ruler; (OE) broad
    ridge
Brody (Gaelic) ditch
Bronislav (Slav.) weapon of glory
Bronley (OE) from brushwood meadow
Bronson (OE) son of dark-skinned man
Bronwen (Celt.) white breast
Brooke (OE) stream
Brooks (OE) dweller by stream
Bruce (Fr., Scot.) woods
Bruno (It., Ger.) brown
Buckley (OE) deer meadow
Buckminster (OE) preacher
Buenaventura (Sp.) well met, adventuring life
Burdett (OFr.) small shield
Burgess (OFr.) bourgeois, citizen
Burke (Teut.) castle
Burl (OE) wine servant
Burnell (OE) brook
Burr (Scand.) youth
Burton (OE) fortress
Busby (Scot.) village on woodlands
Byford (OE) river crossing

Byram (OE) cattle yard
Byron (OFr., Teut.) cottage

C

Cable (OFr.) rope
Cadell (Celt.) strong in war
Cado (Celt., Fr.) war
Cadogan (Celt.) war
Cady (Fr.) dim. Léocadie
Caedmon (Celt., Fr.) wise warrior
Caesar (L) much hair; taken from his mother's womb
Cahit (Turk.) hardworking
Cain (Heb.) craftsman
Cal—short Calvin, Calbert, Calvert
Calbert—var. Calvert
Calder (Celt.) stony river
Cale—var. Caleb
Caleb (Heb.) faithful; (Assyrian) messenger; (Arab.)
    brave
Caled—var. Caleb
    Kale
Callum (Celt.) dove
Calvert (OFr.) herdsman
Calvin (L) bald
    Calvino (Sp.)
Cameron (Celt.) bent nose
Camilo (Sp.) freeborn
    Camillus
Campbell (L) beautiful friend
Candan (Turk.) sincerely, heartily
Canute (Scand., Teut.) hill
    Canut, Knute, Knud
Carel (Dut.) var. Charles

Carlisle (OE) from fortified city, Carlile, Carlyle
Carlton (OE) Carl's town
    Carleton
Carmen (Sp. from L) song; (Heb.) vineyard
Carmine (Heb., It.) vineyard
Carol (Fr.) song of joy
Carr (ONorse) marshy land
Carson (ONorse) son of Carr
Cary (Welsh) stony, rock island
    Carey
Casey (Celt.) brave
Casimir (Pol.) declare peace
    Kasimir; Casimiro (Sp.)
Casio (Sp. from L) protected with a helmet
    Cassius; Kasen (Basque)
Caspar (Persian) horseman; treasure master
    Jaspar
Cato (L) wise
    Catón (Sp.)
Cecil (L) blind; gray eyes
    Cecilio (It.)
Cedric (Welsh) bountiful; (Celt.) leader
Cenon (Sp.) var. Zenon
Cesar (Sp.) Caesar
    Caseareo; Cesare (It.); César, Césaire (Fr.)
Chad (A-S) warlike, warrior
Chaim (Heb.) life
    Haim
Chapman (OE) trader
Charlemagne (Fr.)
    Carlomagno (Sp.)
Charles (OFr.) full-grown; manly
    Carlo (It.); Carlos (Sp.); Karel (Dan., Dut.); Karl
    (Ger., Slav.); Carl, Charley, Charlie
Charlton—var. Charles
Chauncey (OE) church official
Chester (L) fortress
    Chet, Caster

Chet (Thai) brother
Chilton (A-S) town by river
Christian (Fr. from L) Christian
    Cristiano (Sp.); Kristian (Swed.);
    Kerstan (Dut.); Kristo (Slav.); Christen (Fr.);
    Chris
Christopher (Gk.) Christ bearer
    Christobal, Christophe (Fr.); Christoph (Ger.);
    Cristoforo (It.); Kristofer (Swed.); Cristoval
    (Sp.); Krzysztof (Pol.); Kristof, Kester
Chula (Choctaw Indian) fox
Cibran (OFr.) Cypriot
Cicero (L) orator, Roman statesman
Ciprian (L) Cypriot
    Cipriano (Sp.); Cyprien (Fr.)
Ciro—var. Cicero
Clancy (Gaelic) tribe
Clare (Fr.) clear
Clarence (L) clear
Clark (OE) clergyman
Claude (L) lame
    Claude (Fr.); Claudio (It., Sp.)
Claus (Dut., Ger. from Gk.) victory of the people,
    short Nicolaus
Clay (OE) fine-grained earth
    Clayton
Cleavon (OE) cliff
Clemence (Fr. from L) merciful
Clement (L) merciful
    Clemente (Sp.); Kelmen (Basque); Clemens, Cle-
    mentius, Clem, Clemon
Cleon (Gk.) Athenian ruler; (OE) hill
Cleveland (OE) cliff
Cliff (OE) steep bank
Clifford (OE) crossing near cliff
Clifton (OE) town near cliff
Clinton—var. Clifton
    Clint

Clive (OE) cliff
Clovis (Fr.) King of Francs; glorious
    Clodoveo (Sp.)
Clyde—name of river in Scotland; (OE) sheltered place
Coburn (OE) small stream
Coby—short Coburn
Colbert (Fr. from OGer.) fresh, bright
Colborn (OGer.) black bear
Colby (OE) coal town; dim. Colbert, Colborn
Cole—dim. Coleman, Colbert, Colborn
Coleman (OE) coal miner; Colman
Colin (L) dove; (Gk.) victor; (Gaelic) child; dim.
    Nicolas
    Colan, Colon, Collin
Conan (Celt.) wisdom
Conn—var. Conan
Connal (Celt.) courageous
Connor—var. Conan
Conon (Fr.) daring
Conrad (Ger.) bold, wise counselor
    Conradin (Fr.); Curt, Kurt, Kord (Ger.); Conrado
    (Sp.); Corradino, Conrard, Radel, Keno
Conroy (Celt.) wise
Constantine (L) constant
    Constantino (Sp.); Constantin (Fr.); Konstanty
    (Pol.); Kosta, Costa
Corbert (OFr.) raven
    Corbin, Corby
Cordell (OFr.) rope
Corentin (Celt., Fr.) friend
Corey (Gaelic) ravine; (A-S) chosen one
Cork—county in Ireland
Cornelius (OFr.) crow; (L) horn
    Cornelio (Sp.); Korneli (Basque); Corneille,
    Cornille (Fr.)
Cornell—var. Cornelius
Cort (Dan., Teut.) bold speech
Corwin (L) raven
Coskun (Turk.) overflowing

Cosmo (Gk.) order, universe
Courtney (L) court
    Court, Courtland
Craig (Celt.) crag
Crandall (OE) crane valley
Crane (OE) cry
Creighton (OE) creek
Crestin (Fr.) var. Christian
    Chrestin, Christin, Krestin
Crispin (L) curly
Cullen (Celt.) cub
Cunaud (Fr., Ger.) strong ruler
    Cunault, Cunwald
Curren (Gaelic) hero
Curt—dim. Curtis; var. Conrad
Curtis (OFr.) courteous
Cuthbert (Fr., Ger.) hero
Cybard (Fr. from Gk.) ruler, saint name
Cyr (Fr. from Gk.) master
    Cyran
Cyril (Gk.) lord
    Cyrille (Fr.); Kiril (Russ.);
    Cirilo (Sp.); Kuiril (Basque); Cirilus
Cyrus (Persian) king, sun
    Ciro (Sp.); Kuir (Basque)

D

Dabert (Fr. from OGer.) bright action
Dabi (Basque) David
Da-chun (Chinese) long spring
Dacy (Fr.) from Arcy, in France
Dag (Teut.) day
Dagan (Heb.) grain, Babylonian god of the earth
Dagny (Teut.) fresh as day

Dagobert (Fr. from OGer.) bright day
    Dagbert, Daibert, Dagoberto (Sp.)
Dahab (Arab.) gold
Daif (Arab.) guest
Daimon (L) guardian angel
Dale (ONorse) valley
Dalmace (Fr. from L) Dalmatian
    Dalmas, Dalmaso, Dalmo
Dalton (OE) farm in the valley
Damian (Gr.) taming
    Damieno, Damien; Damián (Sp.); Damen
    (Basque)
Damon (Fr.) son of Hamon; classical legend, friend of
    Pythias
Dan (Heb.) judge
Dana (Scand.) Dane
Dani (Heb.) my judge
Daniel (Heb.) God is my judge
    Daniel (Fr., Sp.); Danilo, Deniel, Danielo (Sp.);
    Danel (Basque)
Dante (It.) lasting
Dar (Heb.) pearl
Daracy (Irish, OFr.) from Arcy
Darby (Fr.) from Arby, in France; (Irish) freeman;
    (ONorse) deer park
Darcy (Irish, OFr.) from Arcy; (Gaelic) dark
    Darcey, Darcet, Darsy
Darian (A-S) dear, darling; (Persian) wealthy
    Darius, Darin, Darren, Dorian, Darrell, Daryl,
    Darrol
Darioush (Persian) ancient king
Darlan (Fr.) son of Arland or Arlot; (OGer.) army
    Darlot
Daron (Gaelic) great
    Darren
Darrel (OE) beloved
    Darryl, Daryle
Darson (Fr.) son of Arson (hatmaker)

Datan (Pol.) mythological god of abundance

Dauphin (Fr.) dolphin, dauphin (eldest son of king of
    France)
    Delphin

Daurian (Fr.) var. Dorian; (L) golden

Davi—short David

David (Heb.) beloved
    Davin, Davi, Dave, Davey, David (Fr., Sp.); Dabi
    (Basque)

Davis (Scot.) David's son
    Davidson, Davison

Davorin (Slav.) god of war

Dawid (Pol.) David

Dawit (Ethiopian) David

Dawud (Arab.) David
    Daud

Da-xia (Chinese) long summer

Dean (L) presiding official; (OE) from the valley

Dekkel (Arab.) palm tree

Delano (OFr.) of the night

Delmore (Fr.) of the sea
    Delmar, Delmor

Delwin (Teut.) valley friend

Deman (Dut.) man

Demetrius (Gk.) var. Demeter, goddess of harvest

Demonthin (Ponca Indian) talks as he walks

Deniau (Fr.) var. Daniel; also son of Niel
    Deniel, Daniau

Denis (Fr.) Dionysus, Greek god of wine
    Denys, Dennis, Nissot

Denton (OE) valley farm

Deon (Fr.) god
    Deom, Dione

Derek (OGer.) people's wealth
    Derrick, Derk, Dirk

Derlen (Celt., Fr.) oak tree

Dermot—var. Darby; (Gaelic) free from envy
    Diarmid

Deron (Heb.) freedom; bird (swallow)
Desiderio (Sp.) desired
Desmond (Irish) clan name, from South Munster
Detlef (Ger.) descendant
Devir (Arab.) holy place
Dewi—var. David
Dexter (L) dexterous
Dia-Allah (Arab.) light of God
Didier (Fr.) desired, beloved
Diego (Sp.) James
Diel (Fr.) worshiper of God
Dieterich (Ger.) people's rule
    Ditrik, Dietland, Didrich, Dieter, Dietrich, Dytrych, Dirk, Dierk, Didry; Thierry, Thiéry, Theriot (Fr.)
Dillon (Gaelic) faithful; (OGer.) people
Dinko (Slav.) Sunday's child
Dinos (Gk.) constant
Dion (Gk.) var. Dionysos
Diosdado (Sp.) Godgiven
Dipak (Hindi) lamp, moonlight
Dirk (Teut.) dagger; var. Derek, Dieterich
Dishon (Heb.) antelope
Djamal (Arab.) beauty
    Jamal, Gamal
Dmitri (Russ.) var. Demeter
    Dimitri
Dodd (Teut.) of the people
Domitien (Fr. from L) conqueror
    Domitian, Domitius
Domonic (L) Lord
    Dom, Dominick, Dominique (Fr.); Domingo (Sp.); Domiku (Basque); Dominico, Domenico (It.)
Donald (Celt.) proud chief; (Irish) dark stranger
    Donal, Doughal
Donar (OGer.) mythological god of thunder
Dor (Heb.) generation, dwelling

Doran (Celt.) stranger

Dore (Gk.) Isidore

Dorian (Gk.) name of ancient people of Doris; var. Darian

Doron (Heb.) gift

Douglas (Celt.) dark stranger, dark stream
Dougal, Dowal

Dov (Heb.) bear

Drake (OE) male duck

Drew—short Andrew; (OGer.) carrier; (OFr.) sturdy; (Gk.) vision; (Welsh) wise; (Teut.) skillful
Dru

Duane (Celt.) song, little dark one
Dwayne

Duarte (Teut.) rich guard

Dudley (OE) people's meadow

Dugald (Celt.) black hair

Dumah (Arab.) silence

Duncan (Gaelic) dark warrior

Dunstan (A-S) brown stone hill

Dur (Heb.) circle

Durosinni (Yoruba, West Africa) stay and bury me (wish for longevity for child)

Durward (Persian) doorkeeper

Duryea (L) lasting

Dustin (OGer.) valiant fighter

Dwight (OGer.) white, fair

Dylan (Welsh) sea

E

Eamon (Irish) fortunate warrior; var. Edmund
Earl (OGer.) intelligent
Earle (A-S) noble
Eaton (OE) riverside village
Eben (Heb.) rock; short Ebenezer
  Eban
Ebenezer (Heb.) rock of help
Edan (Celt.) flame, fiery
Eddy (Scand.) energetic; short Edward, Edgar
Edelin (Fr. from OGer.) noble
  Edelot
Edgar (A-S) happy warrior; (Teut.) rich spear
  Edgardo (It., Sp.); Edouard, Edgard (Fr.); Eduardo (Sp.)
Edison (OE) Edward's son
Editon (Omaha Indian) as a sacred object
Edlin (A-S) prosperous friend
Edmund (A-S) prosperous protector
  Edmundo (Sp.); Edmond, Edmont (Fr.)
Edon (Fr. from OGer.) wolf
Edric (A-S) prosperous ruler
Edsel (A-S) from Ed's hall
Edson (A-S) Ed's son
Edward (OGer.) prosperous, happy guardian
  Ed, Ned, Ted, Teddy; Eduardo (It., Sp.); Ediuard, Eduard (Ger.); Edvard (Scand.); Edouard (Fr.)
Edwin (OGer.) happy friend
  Eduin (Fr.)
Efram (Heb.) fruitful
  Ephraim, Efrem, Ephrem
Efrat (Heb.) honored

Egbert (Teut.) brilliant
Egerton (OE) town on ridge
Eglantine (OFr.) sweetbrier, wild rose
Egon (Celt.) ardent; (Teut.) formidable
    Egan
Egor (Russ.) George
    Igor
Eilard (Fr. from OGer.) strong
Einar (Ger., Nord.) chief, warrior
Elan (Heb.) tree
Elazar (Heb.) God helps
    Elazaro (It.); Elazar (Basque); Lazaro, Eleazar
    (Sp.)
Elbert (Teut.) brilliant
Elden (OE) valley of elves
    Eldon, Elton
Eldred (A-S) wise counselor
    Aldred
Eldridge—var. Eldred, Aldrich
Eldwin (A-S) wise friend
    Aldwin
Eleazor (Heb.) var. Elazar
    Eliezer, Elzaro
Elgar—var. Alger
Elgin (OE) white, noble
Elhanan (Heb.) God is gracious
Elhav (Heb.) gift of God
Eli—var. Ely
Elias (Heb.) Jehovah is God
    Elihu, Elijah, Eliot, Ellis, Ely, Eliet, Eliaz, Elisé
Elihu (Heb.) He is my God
Elijah (Heb.) the Lord is my God
Elio (It., Sp.) var. Helio (Gk.) sun
Eliseo (Heb.) God is my salvation
Elisha (Heb.) God is my salvation
Elishama (Heb.) God hears
Elisheva (Heb.) God is my oath
    Elisheba

Elkan (Heb.) Lord is possessing, God has acquired, belonging to God
    Elkanah
Ellard (Teut.) brave
Ellery (Teut.) alder tree
Elliot—var. Elias
Ellis—var. Elisha
Ellison—son of Elias
    Elson
Elmer (Teut.) famous
Elmo (Gk.) amiable
Elnathan (Heb.) God gives
Elner (Teut.) famous
Eloy (L) worthy to be chosen
    Éloi (Fr.)
Elrad (Heb.) God is my ruler
Elric—var. Aldric
Elroy (L) royal
Elton (OE) old farmstead, town; var. Elden
Elvio (Sp. from L) yellow, blond
Elvis (Nord.) wise
Elwin (A-S) friend of elves
Ely (Heb.) ascend, lifting up, offering
    Eli
Emanuel (Heb.) God is with us
    Emmanuel, Manuelli, Emanuelli (It.); Manuel (Sp.)
Emelin (Teut.) industrious
    Emlyn, Emlin
Emerson—son of Emery
Emery (Teut.) industrious; var. Amery
    Emoré (Fr.); Amerigo (It.); Emmerick (Ger.); Imre (Hung.); Emory, Emeri
Emil (Teut.) energetic
    Emile, Emilion
Emin (Turk.) safe, secure
Emiot (Fr.) var. Amyot
Emmeran (OGer.) raven

Emmet (Heb.) truth; (A-S) diligent
Enayat (Arab.) careful
Endemon (Gk.) fortunate
Endimion (Gk.) mythological figure, son of Jupiter and
    Calyce (nymph), so beautiful, honest and just,
    Jupiter made him immortal
Endrey—var. André, Andrew
Enea (It. from Gk.) ninth
Englebert (OGer.) famous, bright
    Enjalbert, Engelbert (Fr.)
Enoch (Heb.) educated, dedicated
Enos (Heb.) man
Enric (Fr.) var. Henry
    Enrico (It.); Enrique (Sp.); Riquet (Fr.)
Enzo (It.) var. Henry
Ephraim—var. Efram
Ephron (Heb.) fawn
Erasmus (Gk.) amiable
    Erasmo (Sp.); Erasme (Fr.)
Erastus (Gk.) beloved
Erdogan (Turk.) son is born
Erhard (OGer.) honor
Eric (Teut.) brave, powerful, kingly; (ONorse) honor;
    (L) rich
    Erich, Erik, Eryk, Rick, Ricky
Erland (Scand., Teut.) stranger; (OE) noble land
Ernest (OGer.) serious
    Ernst, Ernie, Erno (Hung.); Ernesto (It., Sp.);
    Ernst (Ger.)
Errol (L) wanderer; (Teut.) nobleman
Erskine (Scot.) town name; (Gaelic) height of the cliff
Erwin (OGer.) host, crowd
    Irwin
Evner (Turk.) house
Ewald (OGer.) ruler
Ewen (Celt.) youth
Exupère (Fr., L) surpass
    Exupery

Ezatollah (Arab.) glory of God
Ezekiel (Heb.) strength of the Lord; God will
    strengthen
    Ezechiel
Ezio (It.) aquiline nose; var. Enzo
    Enzio
Ezra (Heb.) help
    Ezer, Ezri, Azur, Azrikam
Ezzat (Arab.) greatness

F

Fabian (L) bean farmer
    Fabiano (It.); Fabio (It., Sp.); Fabien (Fr.)
Fabrizio (It. from L) craftsman
    Fabron, Fabrian (Fr.)
Fadil (Arab.) abundant
Fadoul (Arab.) honest
Fahmy (Arab.) my good understanding
Fairfax (A-S) fair-haired
Faisal (Arab.) wise judge
Fakhri (Arab.) my pride
Falah (Arab.) success
Faleh (Arab.) successful
Falip—var. Philip
Fantin (Fr. from L) child
Farhat (Arab.) joys
Farland (OE) land near road
Farley (OE) bull pasture
    Fairleigh, Farly
Farman (Arab.) decree; (A-S) traveler
Farrell (Celt.) courageous
Farukh (Arab.) young bird
Faruq (Arab.) criterion

Fathi (Arab.) my conquest
Faust (L) fortunate
    Fausto (It., Sp.); Faustin (Fr.)
Fawaz (Arab.) victorious
Fawzy (Arab.) my victory
Faxon (Teut.) thick-haired
Fayad (Arab.) generous
Fayza (Arab.) victorious
Federico (It., Sp.) Fredrick
    Federigo (It.)
Fehmi (Arab.) my knowledge
Felix (L) happy
Fenris—Norse mythological figure
Fenton (OE) town near marsh
Ferdinand (Teut.) adventurous, brave, strong
    Fernando (Sp.); Errando (Basque)
Ferdusi (Persian) paradisical
    Feridoon
Fergus (Celt.) strong
Fernald (Teut.) old alder tree
Feroz (Persian) fortunate
Ferris (Celt.) rock
Feyyaz (Turk.) generous, flourishing
Fidel (Sp.) faithful
    Fidelio (It.)
Fielding (OE) field
Finnian (Celt.) elevation
Firman (OE) fair man
Firmin (L) solid
Fisk (Scand.) fish
Fitzgerald (OE) son of Gerald
Fitzpatrick (OE) son of Patrick
Flaminio (Sp.) Roman priest
Flavio (It., Sp.) blond, yellow
    Flavien (Fr.); Flaviano (Sp.); Palben (Basque);
    Flavius
Fleming (OE) Flanders
Fletcher (OFr.) arrow maker

Florent (Fr. from L) flowering
  Florentin (Fr., Sp.); Florinio, Florentino (Sp.)
Florian (Ger. from L) flowering
Floyd (Celt.) gray
Forbes (Gk.) fodder; (Gaelic) prosperous
Ford (OE) crossing, road
Forrest (L) woodland
Fortuné (Fr.) fortunate
  Fortun (Basque)
Foster (L) forester
Fouad (Arab.) heart
Fowler (OE) gamekeeper
Francis (Teut.) free
  Franco, Francesco (It.); Francisco (Port., Sp.);
  Franz (Ger.); François, Franchot (Fr.); Franciszek
  (Pol.)
Frank—short Francis
Franklin (Teut.) freeman
Frayne (OE) foreigner
Fred—short Frederick
Frederick (Teut.) peaceful ruler
  Fredrick, Friedrich, Friederich, Fredric, Fritz
  (Ger.); Federico (It., Sp.); Federigo (It.); Frédéric
  (Fr.)
Freeland (OE) from free land
Freeman (A-S) free man
Frémond (Fr. from OGer.) peaceful protection
Fulbert (OGer.) abundant
Fulton (A-S) field near town
Fyodor (Russ.) Theodore

G

Gabin (Fr.) var. Gabriel
  Gabino (Sp.); Gabin (Basque)
Gabor (Hung.) hero of God; var. Gabriel
Gabriel (Heb.) God is my strength
  Gabrel, Gabel, Gabrio, Gabrielo (Sp.); Gabriele
  (It.); Gavril, Gabriel (Fr.)
Gachero (Kikuyu, Kenya) investigator
Gad (Arab.) gift, happy; (Heb.) happy, fortunate;
  (Navajo Indian) cedar tree
Gadi (Heb.) my fortune
Gadiel (Heb.) God is my fortune
Gaetano (It.) from Gaete
  Gaetan (Fr.); Kayetan; Gay
Gal (Heb.) wave; mountain
Galard—var. Gaylord
Galdemar (Fr., OGer.) famous ruler
Gale (OE) joyous, lively
Galen (Gk.) calm, tranquil
Galip (Turk.) victorious
Gallien (Fr., L) Roman emperor; (Teut.) stranger,
  foreigner
Galmier (Fr., Teut.) famous ruler
  Galeran
Galo (L) from Gaul
Galt (OE) high land
Galvin (Celt.) sparrow
Gamal (Arab.) beauty
Gamalat (Arab.) beautiful one
Gamaliel (Heb.) God is my judge, God rewards
Gamliel (Heb.) God is my reward
Ganet—var. Gerard

Ganeza—Hindu god of wisdom and intelligence
Garai (Basque) Vincent
Gardell (Teut.) guardian
Gardiner (OFr.) gardener
    Gardner
Garfield (OE) promontory, battlefield
Garland (OFr.) crowned
Garner (Teut.) protecting warrior
Garrett (Teut.) mighty with spear; (OE) great warrior;
    (Welsh) gentle
    Garret, Garreth
Garrick (A-S) oak spear; (Teut.) spear king
    Garik, Garek
Garson (Fr.) young man, garrison
Garth (ONorse) garden, enclosure; var. Garrett
Garvey (A-S) warrior; (Gaelic) hard-won peace
Garvin (Teut.) befriending warrior
Gary—var. Garrett, Garrick, Garvey
Gaspar (Persian) treasure master; (OGer.) host
    Gaspard (Fr.); Gaspardo (It.); Gaspar (Sp.)
Gaston (Fr.) native of Gascony; (OGer.) host
    Gascon
Gaubert (OGer.) brilliant ruler
Gauderic (OGer.) ruler, king
Gautier (Fr.) Walter
    Gauthier, Gaultier
Gavin (Celt.) hawk
    Gauvin (Fr.); Galvano (It.); Gawen
Gaylord (OFr.) joyful, bold
Generoso (Sp.) generous
Geoffrey (Teut.) var. Godfrey; (A-S) gift of peace
    Geoff, Jeff, Jeffrey
George (Gk.) farmer
    Georges (Fr.); Giorgio (It.); Jorge (Sp.); Iorgos
    (Gk.); Georg (Dan., Ger.); Joris (Dut.); Jiri
    (Czech); Jerzy (Pol.); Gheorgui, Yuri, Igor
    (Russ.); Goran (Slav.); Geordie (Scot.); Jorgan,
    Yurik, Jurric, Jurgan
Gerald (Teut.) powerful soldier

Geraldo (It.); Giraldo (Sp.); Gérard, Géraud (Fr.); Gerardo (Sp.), Gerhard, Gerart (Ger.)

Gerard—var. Gerald

Gerland (OGer.) spear of the land

Germain (Fr.) sprout, germane
German (Sp.); Kerman (Basque); Garmon, Guerman, Jermen (Fr.)

Gero (Hung.) watchman

Geronimo (Gk.) holy name

Gershon (Heb.) stranger
Gerson, Gershom, Gersham

Gervais (Fr. from Teut.) warrior
Gervase (Fr.); Gervasio (Sp.); Kerbasi (Basque)

Gery (OGer.) spear

Geva (Heb.) hill
Givon

Ghali (Arab.) precious

Ghislain (Fr. from OGer.) sweet pledge

Giacommo (It.) Jacob

Gian-Carlo (It.) combination John and Charles

Gibor (Heb.) strong

Gichuhi (Kikuyu, Kenya) ring

Gideon (Heb.) mighty warrior
Gidi

Gidie (Ethiopian) mine

Gifford (Teut.) splendid gift

Gil (Heb.) joy; short Gilbert

Gilad (Arab., Heb.) height, man from Giladi (mountain range near Jordan River)
Gilead, Giladi

Gilbert (Teut.) illustrious pledge
Gilberto (It., Port., Sp.)

Gilen (Basque) Gil

Giles (Gk.) shield bearer; (Teut.) pledge; (L) var. Julius
Gilles

Gilford (OE) from Gill's ford

Gili (Heb.) my joy
Gilli

Gillen (Basque) William
Gillian (L) youth
Gilmer (Teut.) famous pledge
Gilmore (Gaelic) glen near sea
Gilroy (Celt.) servant of king
Gils (Teut.) pledge
Gino (It.) short Louis, Amrose
Ginson (Heb.) garden
    Ginton
Gireg (OGer.) spear
Giusto (It., L) just
Glen (Gaelic) valley
Glendon (Gaelic) dark valley
Goddard (Teut.) divine firmness, God is firm
    Gotthard (Dut., Ger.); Godard, Gothard, God-
    rard (Fr.)
Godfrey (Teut.) God's peace
    Gottfried (Ger.); Godofredo (Port., Sp.); Gof-
    fredo, Godefredo, Giotto (It.)
Godwin (Teut.) divine friend
    Goodwin
Goel (Heb.) redeemer
Goodman (A-S) good man
Goran (Slav.) George
Gordon (Gaelic) hero; (OE) cornered hill
Gore—var. Gregory
Gorka (Basque) George
Gover (Heb.) victorious
Gower (Welsh) virtuous
Goyal (Heb.) bird
Graham—var. Gram
Graig—var. Craig
Gram (L) grain; (A-S) gray home
    Graeme, Graham
Grant (L) great
Grantham (OE) great meadow
Grantland (OE) large meadow
    Grantley

Granvil (OFr.) large town
 Grenville
Grayson (OE) son of bailiff
Greg (Celt.) fierce
Gregor (Gk.) watchman
Gregory (Gk.) watchful
 Grégoire, Grégorie, Grégor (Fr.); Gregorio (It.,
 Port., Sp.); Gregor, Grigor (Ger., Slav.) Gregoor
 (Dut.), Gregorius, Greger, Greer, Gore, Greg,
 Grigori, Joris
Gresham (OE) grassland
Griffin (Welsh) strong in faith
Griswold (Teut.) gray forest.
Grosvenor (Fr.) mighty huntsman
Grover (OE) grove
Gudwal (OGer.) leader in battle
Guerric (OGer.) protector
Guillaume (Fr.) William
 Guillermo (Sp.); Gilamu (Basque)
Gunnar (Norse, Teut.) war
Gunther (OGer.) war
Gur (Heb.) young lion, strength
Guri (Heb.) my lion, my strength
Guriel (Heb.) God is my lion (protector)
Gurion (Heb.) lion, strength
Gustave (Teut.) staff of the gods
 Gustaf (Ger.)
Guthar (Teut.) warrior
Guthrie (Celt.) war serpent
Guy (Celt.) sensible; (Heb.) valley; (L) life; (OFr.)
 guide; (Teut.) warrior
 Guido (It., Sp.)
Gwennin (Celt.) white

H

Haaris (Arab.) vigilant
Habib (Arab.) beloved
Hadar (Heb.) ornament
Hadden (OE) heath
Hadi (Arab.) guide
Hadley (OE) heath-covered meadow
Hadrien—var. Adrien
Hadwin (Teut.) friend in war
Hafiz (Arab.) preserver, one who knows Koran by
    heart
Hagos (Ethiopian) happy
Haines (Teut.) hedged enclosure
Haj (Arab.) sincere, title given to someone who has
    made pilgrimage to Mecca
    Hadj, Haji
Hal—short Harry, Henry, Harold
Halbert (Teut.) bright stone
Halden (Teut.) half Dane
Hale (OE) hall; (Teut.) robust
Haley (ONorse) hero
Halford (OE) manor by the ford
Halim (Arab.) patient
Halit (Turk.) continuous
Hall (OE) hall
Hallam (Teut.) hillside
Haloke (Navajo Indian) salmon
Halsey (OE) from Hal's island
Hamda (Arab.) thankfulness
Hamdan (Arab.) thankful
Hamid (Arab.) praiseworthy
Hamilton (OE) beautiful mountain
Hamlin (OE) var. Henry

Hanafi (Arab.) orthodox
Hanan (Heb.) grace
    Johanan, John
Hananel (Heb.) God is gracious
Hanford (OE) high ford
Hanif (Arab.) orthodox, true
Hanley (OE) meadow
Hans (Ger.) short Johannes
    Hansel
Hanson—var. Johan
Harcourt (Teut.) fortified; (OFr.) court
Harden (OE) hare valley
Hardy (Teut.) strong
Harel (Heb.) mountain of God
    Harrell
Hari (Hindi) name for Lord Vishnu, who sustains the
    world
Harish (Hindi) legendary king of the monkeys
Harlan (Teut.) land of warriors
Harley (OE) hare meadow
Harlow (ONorse) army leader
Harman (OE) soldier
    Harmon
Harold (Teut.) mighty in battle
    Arnaldo, Aroldo (It.); Harry, Hal, Harald
Harris—son of Harry
Harrison—son of Harry
Harry (Teut.) home rule
Hart (OE) deer
Hartley (OE) deer meadow
Hartwell (Teut.) deer spring
Harvey (OFr.) bitter; (OGer.) warrior
    Hervé (Fr.); Hervey
Hashish (Arab.) green grass
Haskell (Heb.) strength, wisdom, understanding; (OE)
    powerful leader; (Yiddish) var. Ezekiel
Hassan (Arab.) handsome
Hayden (Teut.) hedged hill
Hayes (OE) hedged place

Hayward (OE) hedge
Haywood (OE) hayfield
Hector (Gk.) defender, steadfast
    Ettore (It.); Hector (Sp.); Etor (Basque)
Hedi (Arab.) inspired toward the right path
Hega (Omaha Indian) buzzard
Heinrich (Ger.) Henry
Heinz (Ger.) Henry
Helem (Heb.) hammer
Helmar (Teut.) warrior's fury
Heman (Heb.) faithful
Henderson—var. Andrew
Henry (Teut.) ruler of the home
    Enrico (It., Sp.); Enrique (Sp.); Henri (Fr.);
    Hein, Heinz, Heinrich (Ger.); Hendrik (Dut.);
    Henryk (Pol.)
Herbert (Teut.) bright warrior
    Herb, Bert
Herman (Teut.) warrior
    Ermanno (It.)
Hermes (Gk.) messenger god
Hernan (Teut.) adventuring life
    Hernando (Sp.)
Hersh (Yiddish) deer
    Hershel, Herzl, Heshel
Hervé (Fr.) Harvey
Herwin (Teut.) friend in war
Hevel (Heb.) var. Abel; (Assyrian) son
Hezekiah (Heb.) God is my strength
Hilary (L) cheerful
    Ilario (It.); Hilario (Sp.); Ilari (Basque); Hilaire,
    Hillaire (Fr.)
Hillard (OGer.) warrior
    Hilliard
Hillel (Heb.) praised, famous
Hilton (OE) manor on the hill
Himmet (Turk.) support, help
Hiram (Heb.) exalted, noble
Hobart—var. Hubert

Hod (Heb.) splendor, vigor
Holbrook (OE) brook in the dale
Holden (Teut.) kindly
Hollis (OE) holy tree
Holman (Teut.) river island
Holmes—son of Holman
Holt (OGer.) woods
Homer (Gk.) pledge
Honi (Heb.) gracious
Honoré (Fr.) honor
    Honorato (Sp.); Onorata (Basque)
Honovi (Hopi Indian) strong deer
Horace (L) timekeeper
    Horatius, Horaz, Horatio (Ger.); Orazio (It.);
    Horacio (Sp.)
Horton (L) garden
Hosea (Heb.) salvation
Howard (Teut.) guardian
Howell (Welsh) lordly
Howland (OE) hilly land
Hubbard (Teut.) var. Hubert
Hubert (Teut.) bright mind
    Hubert (Fr.); Huberto (Port., Sp.); Uberto (It.);
    Hubbard, Hobart, Hubie, Hugh
Hud (Arab., Heb.) repenting
Hugh (Teut.) heart, mind
    Hugo (Sp.); Ugo (It.)
Humbert—var. Hubert
Hume (ONorse) grassy hill; var. Holmes
Humphrey (Teut.) home peace, supporter of peace
Hunter (OE) huntsman
Huntley (OE) hunter's meadow
Hyman (Heb.) life
    Chaim, Hyam

I

Ian (Scot.) John
Ib (Scand. from Phoenician) oath of Baal
    Ibbot (Scot.)
Ibrahim (Arab.) Abraham
Ichabod (Heb.) glory has departed
Iden (A-S) prosperous
Idriys (Arab.) teacher
Ignatius (L) fiery
    Ignace (Fr.); Ignazio (It.); Ignacio (It., Sp.); Ignaz
    (Ger.); Ignace, Ignasha (Russ.); Ignacy (Pol.)
Igor (Scand.) hero; (Russ.) George
Ikar (Russ.) ancient legendary hero
Ilhan (Turk.) prince, emperor, king
Ilia (Russ.) Elias
Ilit (Aramaic) best
Iliyas (Arab.) Elijah
Illan (Basque) Julian
Imre (Hung.) Emeric, Amery
Inali (Cherokee Indian) black fox
Indra—Hindu mythological god of the heavens
Ingeborg (Scand.) protection
    Ingebor
Ingmar (Scand.) famous
Ingram (Teut.) Ing's raven (Ing—Scand. mythological
    hero)
Innis (Celt.) island
Inocente (Sp.) innocent, harmless
    Inocencio (Sp.); Innocenzio (It.); Innocenz
    (Ger.); Innocent (Fr.); Innokentij (Russ.); Sein
    (Basque)
Ioviano (Cheyenne Indian) yellow hawk
Ira (Heb.) descendant

Iram (Arab.) mountain peak, crown of the head
Irmiyah (Arab.) Jeremiah
Irvin (Celt.) west, white; (Gaelic) handsome; (A-S)
   lover of the sea
   Irving, Irv, Irwin
Irwin (A-S) lover of the sea
   Marvin, Mervin, Merwin
Isa (Arab.) Jesus
   Aissa
Isaac (Heb.) laughter
Isaam (Arab.) noble
Isabelo (Sp.) combination
Isaiah (Heb.) salvation of the Lord
   Isa
Ishmael (Arab., Heb.) God will hear
   Isamël
Ishmawiyz (Arab.) Samuel
Isidor (Gk.) gift
   Isidoro (Sp.); Isidor (Basque); Isidore (Fr.); Izy-
   dor (Pol.)
Iskander (Ethiopian) Alexander
Israel (Heb.) soldier of the Lord, prince of God;
   wrestled with God; fighter, ruler
Issachar (Heb.) there is a reward
Istvan (Hung.) Stephen
Itai (Heb.) friendly
Itiel (Heb.) God is with me
Itzhak (Heb.) Isaac
Ivan (Russ.) John
Iver (Scand.) bowman
Ivo (Teut.) archer
   Yves (Fr.); Ivan, Ivón (Sp.); Ibon (Basque); Ivar
   (Dan.); Ives, Iver
Ivor (Scot., Teut.) bowbearer; (L) ivory
Izak (Pol.) Isaac
Izzat (Arab.) opulent

J

Jaad (Arab.) Gad
Jaalib (Arab.) attracting
Jacinto (Sp. from Gk.) purple flower
    Gasento (Basque)
Jack—short Jacob, John
Jacob (Heb.) protected, supplanter
    Jacques (Fr.); Jacobo, Santiago (Sp.); Jakes,
    Jacobe, Jagoba, Yakue (Basque); Jakob (Ger.);
    Yakov, Jasha (Russ.); James, Jake, Jock, Jack
Jacques (Fr.) Jacob, James
    Jacot, Coco—nicknames
Jael (Heb.) ascent
Jaime (Sp.) James
Jaimie—var. James
Jakousi (Japanese) god of medicine
Jalaal (Arab.) glory
Jaleel (Arab.) majestic
Jalil (Arab.) beneficent
Jaliyl (Arab.) glorious
Jamal (Arab.) grace, beauty
James (Heb.) supplanter
    Jim, Jimmy, Jaimie
Jamil (Arab.) beautiful
Jan—dim. James; var. John
Janos (Hung.) John
Janssen (Scand.) John's son
Japhet (Heb.) youthful, beautiful
Jared (Heb.) descendant, ruler
    Jordan, Jori, Jory
Jaron (Heb.) sing out, cry out
Jarratt (Teut.) strong spear
Jarvis (OE) driver; (OGer.) sharp spear

Jasha (Russ.) Jacob
Jason (Gk.) healer
Jasper (Heb.) precious stone; var. Caspar
    Jaspar, Caspar, Gaspar
Javier (Basque) new house; var. Janvier (Fr.) January
    Xavier, Javier (Sp.)
Jay (OGer.) lively, bird
Jean (Fr.) John
Jed (Heb.) short Jedidiah; (Arab.) hand, star
Jedidiah (Heb.) beloved of the Lord
Jeffrey (Teut.) God's peace
    Jeff, Geoffrey
Jehan—var. John
Jehiel (Heb.) may God live
    Yechiel
Jehoiakim (Heb.) God will establish
    Akim (Russ.); Joachim; Joaquin (Sp.)
Jephtah (Heb.) he will open (name for first born or
    eldest)
Jeremiah (Heb.) God will uplift
    Jerold; Jeremias (Sp.); Jeremi (Basque)
Jeremy—var. Jeremiah
Jerome (Gk.) sacred name
    Jerry, Gerome, Jeronimo, Geronimo, Hieronymo;
    Jerónimo (Sp.) Jerolin (Basque)
Jerrold (Teut.) mighty with spear
    Gerald
Jerzy (Pol.) George
Jesse (Heb.) grace of God, God exists, gift, wealthy
    Jess
Jesus (Heb.) God saves
Jethro (Heb.) abundance
Jiaan (Persian) strong
Jiri (Czech.) George
Joab (Heb.) willing, God is father
Joachim—var. Jehoiakim
Job (Heb.) symbol of piety and resignation of the just,
    faced with trials
Jochanan (Heb.) God is gracious

Jocheved (Heb.) God is glorious
    Jochebed
Jodel (L) sportive
Jodi—var. Judah
    Jody
Joel (Heb.) Jehovah is God
John (Heb.) God's gracious gift
    Jean (Fr.); Sean (Irish); Ian (Scot.) Jon, Jonathan
    (Heb.); Jochanan, Johanan, Johan, Jochan, Johannes (Ger.); Giovanni (It.); Jon (Basque); Ivan
    (Russ.); Jan, Hans (Dut., Ger.)
Johnston (Scot.) son of John
    Johnson
Jol (Basque) Joel
Jonah (Heb.) dove, God gives
    Jonas
Jonathan (Heb.) God gives
Joran—var. George
Jordan (Heb.) descendant
    Jourdain (Fr.)
Jorens (Norse) laurel
Jorgen (Dan.) George
Jorin (Sp. from Heb.) child of freedom
Joris—var. George
Joseph (Heb.) God will add
    José (Sp.), Giuseppe (It.); Josko, Joska (Slav.);
    Yusuf (Arab.); Josep, Josef (Pol.); Josce (OFr.);
    Pepe, Pepito (Sp. nicknames); Beppo, Peppo (It.
    nicknames)
Joshua (Heb.) God saves, whose salvation is the Lord
    Josh; Josué (Fr., Sp.); Jesus; Josu, Yosu (Basque)
Josiah (Heb.) the Lord heals, supports; (Arab.) God
    has protected
Josse (Fr.) var. Jesse
    Josselin (Fr.)
Jothan (Swiss) John; (Heb.) God is perfect
    Jotham (Heb.)
Jovan (Swiss) John
Joyce (OFr.) joyful

Juaud (Arab.) generous, horse
Jud—var. Judah
Judah (Heb.) praise
    Jud, Judd, Jude, Juda, Judas, Juddah
Jude—var. Judah
Judicaëld (Celt.) God is generous
Jules (L) youthful
Julian (L) youthful
Julius (L) youthful
    Julio (Sp.); Yuli (Basque); Jule (Fr.); Juliusz (Pol.)
Junius (L) youthful
Jurden—var. Jordan
Juri (Slav.) George
Justin (L) just
Justinien (Fr.) var. Justin
Juvénal (Fr. from L) youth

K

Kadeg (Celt.) combat
Kadmiel (Heb.) God is the ancient one
Kadri (Arab.) my destiny
Kaëlig—var. Judicaël
Kai (Scand. from Celt.) combat
Kalil (Heb.) crown
Kaliym (Arab.) speaker, orator
Kalle (Swed. from Teut.) man
Kama (Thai) gold
Kamal (Arab.) perfect
    Kamil
Kammu (Hindi) nickname Kanwal
Kane (Celt.) bright, fair
    Kayne
Kaniel (Arab.) spear; (Heb.) need

Kano—Japanese god of waters
Kanwal (Hindi) lotus
Karel (Dan., Dut. from Teut.) strong man
    Karol (Pol.); Karoly (Hung.)
Karim (Arab.) generous
    Kareem
Karsten (Slav.) Christian
Kasem (Thai) happiness
Kasper (Persian) treasure master
    Caspar, Jaspar, Gaspar
Katriel (Heb.) crown of the Lord
Kauldi (Basque) Claude
Kaveh (Persian) ancient hero
Kaye (Gk.) rejoicing; (Teut.) fortified place; (L) merry
    Kay
Kean (Irish) vast
Keane (OE) sharp; (Celt.) tall, handsome
Kedar (Arab.) black, dark-skinned
Kedem (Heb.) ancient; from the East
Keegan (Celt.) contraction MacEgan (son of Eagan—
    fiery)
Keenan (Gaelic) little ancient one; (OE) wise
Keir (Teut.) ever king; (Celt.) dark-skinned
Keith (Celt.) forest, battlefield
Kellile (Ethiopian) my protection
Kelly (Teut.) farm by the spring
Kelmen (Basque) Clement
Kelsey (Teut.) dweller by the water
Kelton (Celt.) Celtic town
Kelvin (Celt.) narrow river
Kendal (Celt.) bright valley
Kenley (OE) king's meadow
Kenneth (Celt.) handsome
    Ken
Kenric (A-S) bold ruler
    Kendric
Kent (Celt.) white, bright
Kenton (OE) farmstead at Kent
Kenway (A-S) courageous

Kenyon (Gaelic) blond, white-haired
Kermit (Celt.) var. Dermot, Diarmud
Kerry (Celt.) dark
    Keary, Kerrie
Kerwin (Celt.) dark-skinned
Kester (L) of the Roman camp; (Gk.) var. Christopher
Keturah (Heb.) fragrance
Kevin (Celt.) kind
Keyne (Celt.) beauty
Khalid (Arab.) immortal
Khalipha (Arab.) successor
Khamis (Arab.) army, Thursday
Khayam (Arab.) tent maker
Kieren (Celt.) black
Kilby (Teut.) farm by the spring
Kilian (Celt.) Cecil
Kimane (Kikuyu, Kenya) big bean
Kimball (A-S) brave
King (OE) king
Kingdon (OE) king's hill
Kingsley (OE) king's meadow
Kingston (OE) king's manor
Kirby (Teut.) church village
Kirill (Russ.) Cyril
Kirin (L) spearman
Kirk (Teut.) church
Kishen (Hindi) name for Lord Krishna
Kitron (Heb.) crown
Kjol (Norse) people's wolf
    Kjold
Klas (Ger.) short Nicolas
    Klaus
Kléber (Fr.) name of French general
Klemen (Hung.) Clement
Knud (Scand.) kind, race
Kobla (Ewe tribe, Ghana) Tuesday's child
Kodzo (Ewe tribe, Ghana) Monday's child
Kofi (Ewe and Ashanti tribes, Ghana) Friday's child
Kolbjorn (Scand.) black bear

Konan (Teut.) bold
Kondratij (Russ.) bold council
Konrad (Teut.) able in counsel
Konstanty (Pol.) Constantine
Korah (Heb.) bald
Kornel (Dut.) Cornell
Kosi—Congolese god of the waters
Koste (Slav.) Constantine
Kovit (Thai) expert
Kristof (Swiss) Christopher
    Kristofer, Kryslof
Kryiakos (Gk.) Sunday's child
Krzysztof (Pol.) Christopher
Ksawery (Pol.) Xavier
Kub (Pol.) Jacob
    Kuba
Kumar (Hindi) prince
Kunel (OGer.) bold speech
    Kunat
Kurt (Teut.) bold speech; dim. Konrad
Kwabena (Ashanti tribe, Ghana) Monday's child
Kwaku (Ewe and Ashanti tribes, Ghana) Wednesday's child
Kwame (Ashanti tribe, Ghana) Saturday's child
Kwao (Ewe tribe, Ghana) Thursday's child
Kwasi (Ewe and Ashanti tribes, Ghana) Sunday's child
Kyle (Celt.) combat
Kynan (Welsh) chief

L

Laban (Heb.) white
Labid (Arab.) intelligent
Ladislo (It., Slav.) famous ruler
　　Ladislas (Fr.); Ladislav
Laird (Scot.) wealthy landowner
Lakshman (Hindi) younger brother of Ram
Lambert (Teut.) country's brightness
　　Lamberto (It.); Lambrecht (Ger.)
Lamont (Scand.) lawyer
Lance (OGer.) land; short Lancelot
Lancelot (L) servant
　　Lancilotto (It.)
Landers (OFr.) grassy plain
　　Landris
Landon (OE) long hill
　　Langdon
Landry (A-S) ruler
Landwin (Teut.) friend of the country
Lane (OE) lane
Lanfrance (It. from Teut.) free country
Lang (Teut.) long
Langley (OE) long meadow; (OFr.) Englishman
Langston (OE) long town
Lann (Celt.) sword
Laris (L) cheerful
Lars (Swed.) Lawrence
Laserian—var. Lazare
Latham (Teut.) dweller by the barn
Lathrop (A-S) village
Latimer (OFr.) Latin interpreter
Laurence (Fr. from L) laurel

Lautaro (Sp.) Chilean hero who fought against the Spanish

Lavi (Heb.) lion

Lawrence (L) laurel
> Laurence, Laure, Laurentin, Laurent (Fr.); Lorenzo (It.); Lorenço (Port.); Laurens (Scand.); Lars (Swed.); Loritz, Lauritz (Dan.); Lorenzo (Sp.); Lauran, Llorentz (Basque)

Lawton (OE) hillside farm

Lazare (Fr., Heb.) God will help
> Lazarro (It.); Lazaro, Lazarillo (Sp.); Elazar (Basque); Lasar (Russ.); Lazar (Hung.)

Lazarus (Gk., Heb.) God helps

Lazhar (Arab.) best appearance

Leal (L, OFr.) faithful

Leander (Gk.) lion man, courageous
> Léandre (Fr.); Leandro (It., Sp.); Leandros (Gk.); Lander (Basque)

Lech (Pol.) woodland spirit

Ledyard (Teut.) nation's guardian

Lee (L) lion; (OE) meadow; (Celt.) gray; (OE) shelter; short Leland, Leander
> Leigh

Leger (Teut.) people's spear

Leif (Scand.) beloved, descendant

Leigh—var. Lee

Leith (Celt.) wide; (Scot.) river

Lek (Thai) small person (nickname)

Leland (OE) meadowland

Lemuel (Gk., Heb.) dedicated to God

Leo (L) lion
> Léo, Léonce, Léocadie (Fr.); Leon, Leonid, Lev (Russ.); Leonide (Fr., Russ.); Leonidas (Sp.); Lavoslav (Slav.); Leandros (Gk.); Leander

Leonard (Teut.) brave as a lion
> Leonardo (It.)

Leopold (Teut.) patriotic
> Leopoldo (Sp.); Lopolda (Basque)

Leor (Heb.) I have light
Leroy (L) royal
Lesharo (Pawnee Indian) chief
Leshem (Heb.) precious stone
Leslie (Celt.) gray fort
    Lesley
Lester (L) camp of the legion
    Leicester
Lev (Russ.) lion; (Heb.) heart
    Lav, Lew, Leon, Lionel
Liébert (Fr. from OGer.) bold people
Lincoln (Celt.) settlement by the pool
    Linc, Link
Lindley (OE) linden-tree meadow
Lindsay (Teut.) island of serpents
Lionel (L) lionlike
Liron (Heb.) song is mine
Lisandro (It.) var. Alexander
Livingstone (OE) beloved son's place
    Livingston
Llewellyn (Celt., Welsh) lightning, lionlike, ruler
Lloyd (Celt.) gray
Lobo (L, Port.) wolf
    Jean-Loup (Fr.)
Lockwood (OE) enclosed wood
Loman (Celt.) enlightened
Lombard (Teut.) long beard
Lon (Basque) Leon; also dim. Alonso
Lorenzo (It., Sp.) Lawrence
Lorimer (L) harness maker
Loring (OGer.) famous in war
Lot (Heb.) veiled
Lotan (Heb.) protection
Lothar (Ger.) Louis, Luther
Louis (Teut.) famous holiness, famous in battle
    Luis, Ludovico (Sp.); Luigi, Luigino (It.); Louis,
    Ludovic (Fr.); Ludwig (Ger.); Ludvik (Pol.); Luki
    (Basque); Lewis, Lou, Louie, Lothar, Lothair

Loup (Fr.) wolf
Lourdes (Sp.) shrine of Virgin Mary
Lowell (OE) beloved
   Lovell
Lubin (Teut.) love and friend
Luc (Fr. from L) light
   Lucio (It.); Lucien, Lucain, Lucin, Jean-Luc (Fr.);
   Lucas (Sp.); Luk (Basque); Lucius
Lucero (Sp. from L) brings light
Lucius (L) light
   Lucian, Luciano (It.)
Ludlow (OE) prince's hall
Lut (Arab., Heb.) hidden
   Lot
Lütfü (Turk.) gracious
Luther (Teut.) famous warrior
   Lothaire (Fr.); Lotario (It.); Lothar (Ger.)
Lydell (OE) open dell
Lyle (L) island
   Lisle
Lyman (OE) valley
Lyndon (Teut.) linden-tree hill
Lynn (A-S) cascade
   Lin, Linn
Lysander (Gk.) liberator

M

Mac (Celt.) son
Macaire (Fr. from Gk.) happy, blessed
   Macario (It.); Makarios (Gk.)
Macklin (Celt.) contraction MacFlann—son of Flann
   (red-haired)
Macnair (Gaelic) son of the heir
Madaan (Arab.) striving

Maddock (Celt.) fire
    Maddox
Madjid (Arab.) glorious
    Majeed, Majid, Magied
Magloire (Fr.) my glory
Maher (Arab.) clever, skilful; (Heb.) excellent, indus-
    trious
Mahfuz (Arab.) guardian
Majnoon (Persian) legendary hero like Romeo (story
    of Majnoon and Leila)
Makya (Arizona Hopi Indian) eagle hunter
Mal (Teut.) work; dim. Malcolm
Malachai (Heb.) my messenger
    Malachy
Malak (Arab.) angel
Malcolm (Celt.) servant of St. Columbia; (Arab., L)
    dove
Malik (Arab.) king
Malkawn (Heb.) their king
Malkin (Heb.) bitter
Mallory (OFr.) ill omen; (OGer.) war counsel
Mamoun (Arab.) trustworthy
Manassa (Arab.) causes to forget
Mandel (OFr.) cloak maker
Manfred (OGer., Teut.) man of peace
Mansoor (Arab.) victorious
Manton (A-S) estate of king's man
Manuel—short Emmanuel
    Manuelo (It.); Manuel, Manuelito (Sp.)
Manvil (L) great estate
    Manvel
Marc (Fr.) Mark
Marcus (L) hammer; god of war, Mars
Marien (Fr. from L) sea; also var. Marie, Marion
    Marin (Fr.); Mariano (Sp.); Maren (Basque)
Marino (It. from L) sea
Marius (L) Mars, sea
Marjan (Arab.) small pearls
Mark (L) hammer; god of war, Mars

Marcel, Marcellin, Marceau (Fr.); Marcello, Marcelino, Marco, Marciano (It.); Mario (It., Sp.); Marek, Marceli (Pol.); Marius, Marcus

Marland (OE) boundary

Marlow (OE) hill by the lake

Marsden (OE) marsh valley

Marshal (OFr.) officer

Marston (OE) farm by the pool

Marten (Dut., Swed.) var. Mark

Martin—var. Mark

Marvin (Teut.) sea friend
Marwin

Maskil (Heb.) enlightened, educated

Maso (It.) short Tomaso

Mason (OFr.) stoneworker

Masoud (Arab.) very lucky

Mathias—var. Matthew

Matmon (Heb.) treasure

Matok (Heb.) sweet

Matthew (Heb.) gift of God
Mathew, Mathias, Mattathias, Mathieu (Fr.); Mateo (Sp.); Matteo (It.); Matthias (Fr., Swed., Swiss); Matthaus, Mathi (Ger.); Matthia (Gk.); Matai (Basque)

Mattin (Basque) Martin

Maurice (Fr. from L) Moorish
Maurizio (It.); Mauricio (Port., Sp.); Mauro (Sp.); Maurids, Maurits (Dut.); Morey, Morris

Max—short Maximillian, Maxim, Maxwell

Maxime (Fr. from L) greatest

Maximillian (L) greatest

Maxwell (A-S) from Maccus' spring; var. Marcus

Mayer (Heb.) one who shines; (Ger.) overseer, farmer
Meir, Meyer

Maynard (Teut.) mighty firmness
Meinhard (Ger.); Meynard

Medwin (Teut.) powerful

Meged (Heb.) goodness

Mehdi (Arab.) inspired toward the right path
Mehmet (Turk.) Mohammed
Mehr (Persian) sun, love
Mehrdad (Persian) gift of the sun
Mehrzad (Persian) created with love
Meino (Ger.) strong
    Meinbert—strong brightness
    Meinfred—strong peace
    Meinhard—strong firmness
    Meinrad—strong counsel
Mekuria (Ethiopian) pride
Melchior (Heb.) king
Meldon (OE) hillside mill
Melville (Celt.) servant, chief
    Melvin, Malvin
Menachem (Heb.) comforter
Menassah (Heb.) causing to forget
Mendel (Yiddish) var. Menachem
Mengesha (Ethiopian) kingdom
Mercer (Fr.) merchant
Meredith (Welsh) protector from the Sea
Meron (Heb.) army
Merrick—short Almeric
Merton (A-S) farm by the sea
Mervyn (Celt.) sea gull
Merwin (Teut.) friend of the sea
    Merwyn
Meryll (Fr. from OGer.) king
Meven (Celt., Fr.) agile
Michael (Heb.) who is like God
    Michel, Michon (Fr.); Miguel (Sp.); Michaelo,
    Michel (It.); Michail (Slav.); Misha (Russ. dim.);
    Mikel (Basque); Mitchell, Mike, Mickey
Midyan (Arab.) rule, judgment
    Midian
Mieczysław (Pol.) glorious sword
    Miécislas (Fr.)
Mihriban (Turk.) tender, affectionate

Mika (Ponca Indian) raccoon
Mikasi (Omaha Indian) coyote
Mikoali (Pol.) Nicholas
Milan (Gk.) crusher
 Miles, Milo
Milari (Slav. from L) cheerful
Milburn (OE) millstream
Miles (L) soldier
 Myles, Milo
Millard (OE) mill caretaker
Miller (L) miller; (OE) man of the mill
Milos (Slav.) pleasant
Miloud (Fr.) var. Emile
Milton (OE) mill farm
Miroslav (Slav.) peace glory
Misrayn (Arab.) limitation
 Mizraim
Mitiku (Ethiopian) replacement
Mladen (Slav.) young
Moayid (Arab.) supporter
Modesto (Sp.) modest
 Modeste (Fr.)
Mohammed (Arab.) prophet, founder Moslem religion
Mohan (Hindi) Lord Krishna
Moïses (Fr.) Moses
Mojahid (Arab.) militant
Mokbil (Arab.) the approaching one
Mokhtar (Arab.) chosen
Monroe (Celt.) red marsh
 Munro
Monsa (Osage Indian) arrow shaft
Montague (L) peaked mountain
Montega (Osage Indian) new arrows
Moran (Celt.) sea
Mordecai (Heb.) Babylonian god of creation
Moreland (OE) moor
Morely (OE) meadow on the moor
Morrell (L) dark

Morris—var. Maurice
Mortimer (Fr.) still water
Morton (OE) farm on the moor
Morven (Celt.) mariner
Mosha (Heb.) salvation
Moshe (Heb.) saved from the water
    Moïses (Fr.); Moises (Port.); Mousa (Arab.);
    Moses, Moyse, Moss, Moy
Moustapha (Arab.) chosen
    Mustapha
Mubarak (Arab.) blessed
Munir (Arab.) illuminating, bright
Murdoch (Scot.) sea protector; (Celt.) prosperous sea-
    man
Mureithi (Kikuyu, Kenya) herdsman
Murray (Celt.) seaman
Musa (Arab.) mercy; also Moses
Muturi (Kikuyu, Kenya) blacksmith
Mwanaisha (Kikuyu, Kenya) finished person
Myron (Gk.) fragrant

N

Nabil (Arab.) noble
Nadim (Arab.) repentant
Nadir (Arab.) rare, precious
Nadiv (Heb.) noble
Nafis (Arab.) precious
Naftali (Heb.) wreath
    Naftalie
Nagid (Heb.) prince
Nahir (Aramaic) light
Nahum (Heb.) compassionate, comforted
Naib (Heb.) substitute

Najdat (Arab.) he helps
Naji (Arab.) wholesome
    Najib
Najibullah (Arab.) God-given intelligence
Najmuddine (Arab.) star of faith
Nalbert (Fr.) var. Norbert
Naldo (Sp.) contraction Ronald
Namah (Heb.) beautiful
    Naman
Namid (Chippewa Indian) dancer
Namir (Heb.) leopard
Nandel (Ger.) adventuring life
Nansen (Scand.) son of Nancy
Narciso (Sp.) Narcissus
Narcissus (Gk.) daffodil
Nardin (Fr.) var. Bernard
Narkis (Basque, Russ.) Narcissus
Nash (OFr.) cliff
    Ness
Nashif (Arab.) hard
Nashoba (Choctaw Indian) wolf
Nasi (Arab.) pure, sincere
Nasim (Persian) breeze
Nasrollah (Arab.) victory of God
Nassar (Arab.) helper
    Nasir
Nassef (Arab.) just
Nastagio (It. from Gk.) resurrection, Anastasius
Nath (Hindi) god
Nathan (Heb.) gift of the Lord
    Nathaniel, Nathalan, Nat, Nate
Nathar (Arab.) spreading
Nawaab (Arab.) representative
Nduati (Kikuyu, Kenya) gourd of beer
Neal (Celt.) chief; (OE) champion
Necati (Turk.) salvation
Ned (Teut.) rich guard; dim. Edward
Nedelko (Slav.) Sunday's child
    Nedo, Nedan

Nehemiah (Heb.) God comforts
Neil (Celt.) champion
Niels (Scot.); Niel (Dan.); Nels (Scand.); Niels, Nelson, Nealon
Neilson—son of Neil
Nelson—son of Neil, Nel
Nemesio (Sp. from L) justice
Nemiah—var. Nehemiah
Nerée (Fr.) ancient god of the sea
Nero (L) strong, black
Nestor (Sp. from Gk.) wise, old, remembered
Neven (OE) middle
Nevin, Nevins
Nevil (OFr.) new village
Neville
Nevin (Teut.) nephew
Newbold (OE) town near tree
Newell (L) new
Newland (A-S) new land
Niland
Newlin (Celt.) new spring
Newlyn
Newtown (A-S) new estate
Ngwe Khaing (Burmese) silver sprig
Nicanor (Sp. from Gk.) victorious
Nicholas (Gk.) victory of the people
Nicolas (Fr.); Nicolo, Nicola, Cola, Niccolo (It.); Nicol (Scot.); Nicolaas (Dut.); Nikki, Niles (Finnish); Niklas, Nils (Swed.); Nicolau (Port.); Nicolai, Nikita (Russ.); Nicoline, Nikolaos (Gk.); Kolya (Russ. dim.); Nikola (Slav.); Klaus, Nikolaus, Nicolaus, Nicol, Claus, Nilo (Ger.); Mikolas (Basque); Mikolaj (Pol.); Nick, Nicky, Colin
Nicodemus (Gk.) conqueror of the people
Nicodème (Fr.)
Niel (Heb.) pet Nathaniel; (Norse) Nicholas
Neal
Nigel (L) black hair; (A-S) night; (Irish, Scot.) champion

Nike (Gk.) victory
Niles—son of Neal
Niran (Thai) eternal
Nissi (Heb.) sign
    Nissim, Nissan
Niv (Aramaic) speech
Noah (Heb.) rest, peace
    Noé (Fr.)
Noam (Heb.) sweetness, friendship
Noble (L) famous
Noda (Heb.) famous
Noel (Fr.) Christmas
Noga (Heb.) shining, morning light
Nolan (Celt.) noble, famous; (A-S) north land
    Noland, Nolen
Norbert (OGer.) divine brightness; (Teut.) brightness
    of Njord (god of sailors in Norse mythology)
    Norberto (Sp.)
Norman (Fr. from Teut.) from the North; (OE) from
    Normandy
    Normand (Fr.)
Norris (A-S) Norman's house; (Teut.) man from the
    North; (OFr.) caretaker
North (A-S) man from the North
    Northern
Norton (A-S) north farm
Norval (A-S) northern valley
Norward (Teut.) guardian of the north road
Norwin (Teut.) man from the North
Norwood (OE) north woods
Noureddine (Arab.) light of the religion
Novak (Slav.) new
Nowell—var. Noel, Newell
Nuncio (It. from L) messenger
    Nunzio
Nur (Heb.) fire
Nuri (Heb.) my fire
Nuria (Heb.) fire of the Lord

Nuriel (Heb.) fire of the Lord
Nyle (Irish) Neal; (OE) island

O

Oakes (OE) oak tree
Oakley (OE) field of oak trees, oak-tree meadow
Obadiah (Heb.) servant of the Lord
　　Obed, Obediah
Obe—pet Obadiah
Oberon (OGer.) rich, bright; character of Chaucer,
　　Spenser, Shakespeare
Obi (Ibo, Nigeria) heart, homestead of head of house-
　　hold
Obiechina (Ibo, Nigeria) let our homestead not close,
　　let us live on
Obike (Ibo, Nigeria) strong homestead
Octavio (It., Sp. from L) eighth
　　Octavius, Octavien
Odbert (Dan.) bright otter
Odd (Scand.) otter
Ode—pet Odell
Odell (Irish) odd; (Gk.) melody; (OE) from the dell
Odilon (OGer.) rich
Odin (Norse) mythological creator of the world;
　　(OGer.) rich
　　Odon
Odis—var. Odin
Odo—var. Otto
Ofer (Heb.) young deer
Og—biblical king of Bashan
Ogden (OE) oak-tree valley
Ogier (Fr. from Teut.) holy
Ogima (Chippewa Indian) chief

Olaf (Nordic, Teut.) ancestor's relic; (ONorse) reminder of his ancestor
Olav, Ole, Olin, Olen
Ole—pet Olaf, Oleg, Oliver
Oleg (Russ.) holy
Olin (OE) holly
Olney
Oliver (L) olive, symbol of peace
Oliviero (Port.); Olivieros (Sp.); Olivier (Fr.); Ollie, Ole
Olney (OE) from town of that name
Olvan—var. Oliver
Olympio (Gk.) Olympic
Omar (Arab.) follower of the Prophet; (OGer.) famous
Omer
On (Burmese) coconut
Ona (OE) ash tree
Onny (OE) water near ash tree
Onoré (Fr.) var Honoré
Onur (Turk.) dignity, self-respect
Ophelio (Gk.) help
Oral (L) oral
Orban (Fr. from L) globe
Orde (L) order; (OE) beginning
Ordell—var. Orde
Ordway (A-S) warrior with spear
Oren (Heb.) tree
Orin, Oron
Orestes (Gk.) mountain
Orest
Orien (L) the East
Orin, Oris
Orin (Celt.) white-skinned; var. Oren
Oran, Oren
Orland (Teut.) fame of the land; (L) gold; var. Roland; Orlando (It., Sp.)
Orlo (Gk.) gold

Orman (Norse) serpent, symbol of immortality; (Teut.) mariner
    Ormand, Ormond
Ornette (Heb.) light, cedar tree
Orpheus (Gk.) legendary character
    Orphée (Fr.)
Orson (L) bear
Orton (Teut.) wealthy
Orville (Fr.) gold city
    Orval
Orvin (A-S) brave friend
Osbert (A-S) divine brightness
Osborn (A-S) divine strength
    Osborne
Oscar (Celt.) warrior; (OE) divine spear
    Oskar (Ger.); Osgar (Gaelic)
Osgood (Teut.) divine creator
Osman (A-S) servant of God; (Turk.) founder of Ottoman Empire
Osmond (Teut.) divine protector
    Osmundo (Sp.)
Osric (Teut.) divine ruler
Ossie—pet Osmond, Oswald, Oscar
Oswald (Teut.) divine power; (OE) forest of the gods
    Osvald, Oswaldo
Oswin (OE) friend of god
Otemar (Ger.) rich fame
    Othmar, Otmar
Othello (It. from Teut.) rich
    Otello
Othniel (Heb.) God is my strength
Otis (Gk.) keen hearing
Ottavio (It. from L) eighth
Otto (Teut.) prosperous
Ottokar (Ger.) happy warrior
Otway (Teut.) fortunate in battle
Ouni (Arab.) my help
Owen (Celt.) young warrior, lamb; (Gk.) wellborn

P

Pablo (Sp.) Paul
Paco (Sp.) dim. Francisco
Paddy (Irish from L) noble
Page (Fr.) nobleman's attendant
Paine (L) rustic
    Payne
Palmer (L) palm bearer
Pari (Fr.) fatherly
Park (OE) woodland
Parker (OE) park keeper
Parnet (Gk.) stone; var. Peter
    Parnell
Pascal (Fr.) Easter
    Pascual (Fr.); Pasquale (It.)
Pastor (Sp. from L) spiritual leader, shepherd
Patrice (Fr. from L) noble
Patrick (L) noble
    Pat, Patty, Paddy, Patrick (Irish); Patrice (Fr.);
    Patricio (Sp.); Patrizio (It.)
Paul (L) little
    Paolo (It.); Pablo (Sp.); Paulin (Ger.); Pavel
    (Russ.); Paul (Fr.); Pol, Poul (Scand.)
Paxton (Teut.) traveling trader
    Paxon
Payne (L) countryman
Payton (Scot.) dim. Patrick
    Paton, Peyton
Pedro (Sp.) Peter
Peli (Basque) Felix
Pembroke (Welsh) headland
Per (Scand.) Peter

Percival (Gk.) Perseus, Greek mythological figure
    Percy
Perrin (Fr.) var. Peter
Perry (OFr.) pear tree; dim. Peter
Persis (Gk.) Persian
Peter (Gk.) stone
    Pierre, Pierrot, Perrin (Fr.); Perino, Pero, Piero,
    Pietro (It.); Piet, Pietr (Dut.); Petrace (Ger.);
    Kepa (Basque); Petros (Gk.); Piotr (Slav.); Peder
    (Scand.); Pedro (Port., Sp.); Per (Swed., Swiss);
    Petar, Petr, Pete, Pierce, Pearce, Parnell, Parnett,
    Perry
Phelan (Celt.) wolf
Pheodor (Russ.) Theodore
    Feodor
Philander (Gk.) lover of mankind
Philbert (Teut.) brilliant
Philip (Gk.) lover of horses
    Philippe (Fr.); Felipe (Sp.); Pepe (Sp. dim.); Phil
Phineas (Heb.) oracle
Pieran (Celt.) black
Pierce—var. Peter
    Pearce
Pio (It., Sp. from L) pious
Pippin (Dut. from Teut.) father
Pius (L) pious
Placido (Sp.) serene
    Placide (Fr.)
Plato (Gk.) Greek philosopher
    Platon (Russ.)
Pol (Scand.) Paul
Pollard (Teut.) short-haired
Po Mya (Burmese) grandfather emerald
Ponce (Sp.) fifth son
    Pons (Fr.); Ponzio (It.)
Porphyre (Fr. from Gk.) purple stone
    Porfirio (It., Sp.)
Porter (L) gatekeeper

Po Sin (Burmese) grandfather elephant
Powell (Celt.) descendant of Howell, Welsh king
Pravat (Thai) history
Prentice (L) apprentice
    Prentis
Prescott (OE) priest's dwelling
Pricha (Thai) clever
Prince (L) prince
Prior (OE) head of monastery
    Pryor
Priscilliano (Sp.) the ancient
Proctor (L) agent
Prosper (L) fortunate
    Próspero (Sp.); Posper (Basque)
Purisimo (Sp.) purest
Putnam (A-S) dweller by the pond

Q

Qabil (Arab.) able
Qabiyl (Arab.) possession, Cain
Qadim (Arab.) ancient
Qadir (Arab.) powerful
Qadiy (Arab.) magistrate
Qaim (Arab.) upright
Qamar (Arab.) moon
Qariy (Arab.) reader of the Koran
Qasim (Arab.) divider
Qaysir (Arab.) Caesar
Quentin (L) fifth
    Quintis (L); Quintin (Sp.); Kindin (Basque)
Quinby (Scand.) from queen's estate
Quincy (OFr.) estate owned by the fifth son
Quinlin (Gaelic) strong
Quinn (Celt.) wise; var. Conn

R

Rab (Scot.) Robert
Rabi (Arab.) spring
Rachid (Arab.) wise
    Rasheed
Radburn (OE) red stream
Radcliff (OE) red cliff
Radel—var. Conrad
Radford (OE) red ford
Radhi (Arab.) accepting, resigned
Radi (Arab.) content
Radly (OE) red meadow
Rafael (Sp.) Raphael
Rafe (Teut.) house wolf
    Ralf, Ralph, Randolf, Randolph, Randal
Rafi (Arab.) exalted
Raghib (Arab.) willing
Raheem (Arab.) kind
Ra'id (Arab.) leader
Rainald (Ger.) Ronald; var. Reginald
Rainart (Ger.) strong judgment
    Rainhard (Ger., Hung.); Raynard, Renard, Re-
    nart (Fr.)
Rainer (Ger.) counsel
    Regnier, Ranier, Rainier (Fr.)
Rajan (Hindi) ruler
Rajih (Arab.) excellent
Rakin (Arab.) writer
Raleigh (OE) deer meadow
Ralph—see Raul
Ralston (OE) from Ralph's estate
Rambert (OGer.) bright counsel
Ramdane (Arab.) month in Islamic calendar

Ramesh (Sanskrit) cool ray
Ramiro (Sp.) great judge
Ramón (Sp.) Raymond
Ramsey (Teut.) from Ram's island, strong ram
Randall—see Raul
Randolph—see Raul
Ransom (L) redeem
Raphael (Heb.) divine healer
Rafael (Sp.); Rafaelo, Raffaello (It.); Raf (It. dim.); Ray
Rashid (Arab.) director, pious
Rauf (Arab.) kind
Raouf
Raul (Sp. from Teut.) strong, wise counsel
Ralph, Raoul, Rodolphe (Fr.); Rolf (Ger.); Rulf, Rodolf, Rodolfo (It., Sp.); Rudolphe, Rudolf, Rulf, Rollo, Rollin, Rolph, Rudy, Ralf, Randolph, Randall, Randy, Rand
Rawdon (Teut.) deer hill
Ray (OFr.) king; short Raymond; (Scand.) doe
Rayburn (OE) deer brook
Rayhaan (Arab.) sustenance
Raymond (Teut.) mighty protector
Ray, Raimond (Fr.); Raimondo (It.); Ramon (Sp.)
Reda (Arab.) satisfaction
Ridha
Redmond (Teut.) adviser and protector
Reed—see Reid
Regan (Celt., OFr.) kingly
Reginald (Teut.) wise power
Reynold, Reynolds, Ronald, Reinaldo (Sp.); Reinhold (Ger.); Rinaldo (It.); Ranald, Renaud, Reynaud (Fr.); Reggie, Ron, Ronnie, Ronny
Regis (Fr.) ruler
Reid (OE) red-haired
Reed
Reinfred (Teut.) pure peace
Reinhardt—see Rainart

Remus (L) one of founders of Rome
Remy (Fr.) from Reims, France
    Remi
Renat (Russ.) acronym for technical and agricultural
    revolution, name coined after Russian Revolution
Renato (It.) reborn
Renaud (Fr.) Reginald
Rendell—var. Randolph
René (Fr.) reborn
Renfred (Teut.) peacemaker
Renwick (Teut.) raven's nest
Renzo (It.) laurel; short Lorenzo
Restyn (Welsh) restored
Reuben (Heb.) behold a son
    Rubin, Ruben, Reuven
Rex (L) king
Rexford (OE) king's ford
Reyes (Sp.) kings (reference to Adoration of the Magi)
Reynold—see Reginald
Reza (Arab.) resigned to life, accepting
Rhys (Welsh) warrior
    Rice
Ricardo (Sp.) Richard
Richard (OGer.) powerful ruler
    Riccardo, Ricciardo (It.); Ricardo (Port., Sp.);
    Richard (Fr.); Rick, Rich, Dick, Richie, Rik
Richmond (Teut.) powerful protector
Ridgley (OE) meadow ridge
Ridley (OE) red field
Rifai (Arab.) sublime
Riyadh (Arab.) garden
Roald (Scand.) famous power
Robert (Teut.) shining fame
    Roberto (It., Sp.); Robart, Robard, Rupert, Ru-
    bert, Ruprecht (Ger.); Robert (Fr.); Robin, Rob,
    Robby, Rab, Bob, Bobby
Robin—short Robert; also bird name
Roch (Fr., Ger.) glory
Roderick (Teut.) famous ruler

Roderic, Rodrigue (Fr.); Rodrigo (Port., Sp.);
Edrigu (Basque); Rod, Roddy
Rodman (Teut.) red-haired
Rodney (Teut.) famous
Rodolfo (Sp.) var. Raul
Roger (Teut.) famous warrior
Ruggero, Ruggiero, Rogero (It.); Rogelio (Sp.);
Rudiger (Ger.)
Roland (Teut.) fame of the land
Roldan (Sp.); Rolando (Port.)
Rolf—short Randolph, Rudolph
Rollo—short Rudolph, Raoul
Roman (L) Roman
Román (Sp.); Erroman (Basque); Romano (It.);
Romain (Fr.); Roman (Slav.)
Romaric (Ger.) glorious king
Rombaud (Ger.) bold glory
Romeo (It.) pilgrim to Rome, Shakespearean hero
Romney (L) Roman
Romolo (L, Sp.) fame
Romulo
Romulus (L) strength, power
Ronald (Scot.) var. Reginald
Ronan (Scot.) seal
Ronat, Renan
Rory (Celt.) red
Roy
Roscoe (Teut.) deer forest
Roshan (Hindi) one who gives light
Ross (Teut.) horse, red
Roswell (Teut.) great horse
Roushdi (Arab.) my wisdom
Rowland (Teut.) fame of the land
Roy (OFr.) king; (Celt.) red-haired
Royal (OFr.) kingly
Royce (Fr.) kingly
Royd (Scand.) forest clearing
Royden (OE) king's hill
Rubert (Ger.) Robert

Rudhard (Teut.) famous strength
Rudolph—var. Raul
Rudy—short Rudolph
Rue (Gk.) plant
Rufino (It. from L) red
    Rufus, Rufin
Ruford (OE) red ford
Rumwald (Ger.) glorious leader
Rune (Fr., Ger.) secret
    Runo
Rupert (Teut.) shining fame
Russell (L) red hair
Rutherford (OE) cattle ford
Ryan (Gaelic) little king, strong

S

Saad (Arab.) good luck
Saadoon (Arab.) lucky one
Sabeel (Arab.) the way
Sabin—ancient Italian tribe, Sabine
    Sabino (Sp.); Sabin (Basque)
Sadik (Arab.) truthful
Safa (Arab.) crystal clear
Sahak (Persian) ancient hero
Saiyd (Arab.) lucky
Sakda (Thai) power
Sakeri (Dan.) Zachary
Salamon (Hung.) Solomon
Saleh (Arab.) able, skilled, wholesome
Salih (Arab.) honest
Salim (Arab.) safe, healthy, complete
    Salim, Salih, Salman
Salisbury (OE) fortified stronghold, British Prime Minister

Saliyl (Arab.) descendant
Salvador (Sp.) savior
    Salvian, Salvator (Fr.); Salvadore, Salvatore (It.);
    Xabat (Basque)
Salvestro (It.) woody
Salwa (Arab.) consolation
Sam—short Samuel, Samson
Sami (Arab.) hears
Samir (Arab.) good companion
Samson (Heb.) like the sun
Samuel (Heb.) God hears
    Sam, Sammel, Sampson, Samson, Samuelo, Samel
Samy (Arab.) sublime
Sanborn (OE) sandy brook
Sancho (Sp.) holy, devoted to God
    Sanche (Fr.); Sanz (Sp.)
Sander (Fr.) Alexander
Sanders (Gk.) son of Alexander
    Saunders
Sandes (Persian) mythological figure like Hercules
Sandon (OE) sandy hill
Sandor—var. Alexander
Sandro (It.) short Alexander
Sanford (OE) sandy ford
Sanjiv (Hindi) good person
Sanli (Turk.) glorious, illustrious
San Nyun (Burmese) beyond comparison
Sanson (Fr.) splendid sun
Santiago (Sp.) St. James
    Jakome, Xanti (Basque)
Santos (Sp.) saints, holy
Sanzio (It.) holy
Sardis (Heb.) prince of joy
Sargent (OFr.) officer, guard
Sasha (Russ.) dim. Alexander
Saturnin (Fr.) Saturn
    Saturnino (Sp.); Satordi (Basque)
Saul (Heb.) longed for
    Sol

Savill (OFr.) willow farm
Sawyer (Celt.) lumberjack
Saxon (Teut.) swordsman
Sayed (Arab.) great man, gentleman
Sayeh (Persian) shadow
Schuyler (Dut.) shelter
Scot—Scotsman
Seamus (Celt.) James, Jacob
Searle (Teut.) armed
      Serle
Seaton (OE) town by the sea
Seaver (A-S) victorious stronghold
Sebastian (Gk.) venerable, revered
      Sebastien (Fr.); Sebastiano (It., Sp.); Sebasten
      (Basque); Bastien, Bastian
Sebert (A-S) bright hero
Seif (Arab.) sword
Seifeddin (Arab.) sword of the religion or faith
Seifred (Teut.) conquering peace
Selçuk (Turk.) after Seljuk, founder of eleventh-
      century dynasty
Seldon (Teut.) manor in the valley
Selvaggio (It.) wild
Selwyn (A-S) palace friend
Semeon (Heb., Russ.) obedient
Serafino (Sp. from Heb.) seraph
Serge—short Sergius, Roman name, saint name
      Serguei (Russ.)
Serlo (Teut.) armor
Sernin—var. Saturnin
Servan (L) servant, serf
      Serban (Romanian)
Seth (Heb.) compensation, appointed, third son of
      Adam
Severin (Fr. from L) severe, river in England
      Soren
Seward (A-S) coast guard, conquering protector
Sewell (Teut.) sea hero
Seyed (Arab.) master

Seymour (Fr.) Moorish saint; (Teut.) famous at sea; (OE) tailor
Shafiq (Arab.) kind, compassionate
Shaheen (Arab.) desired
Shahin (Persian) eagle
Shahroukh (Persian) regal
Shamin (Arab.) scent
Shamun (Arab.) Simeon, hearing
Sharai (Heb.) prince
Shauky (Arab.) my eagerness
Shaw (OE) shady grove
Shawn—var. John
    Sean
Shaya (Arab.) striving for God
Sheel Chandra (Hindi) quiet and peaceful
Shelby (A-S) ledge farm
Sheldon (A-S) hill on ledge
Shelley (A-S) ledge meadow
Shepherd (A-S) shepherd
    Shep
Shepley (A-S) sheep meadow
    Shep
Sher (Hindi) lion
Sherard (A-S) brave
Sheridan (Celt.) wild
Sherif (Arab.) noble, honest
Sherlock (OE) fair hair
Sherman (OE) shearer
Sherwood (OE) bright forest
Shirley (OE) white meadow
Shishvi (Hindi) autumn
Shoukry (Arab.) my thanks
Shukriy (Arab.) thankful
Shuwha (Arab.) settling down
Sibert (Fr.) var. Sigebert
Sibley (L) prophetic
Sidde (Teut.) conquering brightness
Sidney (Phoenician) from Sidon, ancient city; St. Denys

Siegfried (Teut.) conquering peace, victorious
    Seifred, Sigfrid (Ger.); Siffredo (It.)
Siegmund (Teut.) conquering protection
    Sigismond (Fr.); Sigismondo (It.)
Sigebert (Ger.) bright victory
Sighard (Ger.) conquering firmness
Sighelm (Ger.) conquering helmet
Sigmar (Ger.) conquering fame
Sigmund—var. Siegmund
Sigrad (Ger.) conquering council
Sigurd—Icelandic hero: (Teut.) conquering guard
Sigvor (Scand., Teut.) conquering prudence
Sigwald (Teut.) conquering power
Sikander (Hindi) Alexander
Silas (L) forest
Silvan (Fr. from L) forest
    Silvain, Silvin, Silvestre, Silvester (Fr.); Silvano,
    Silvio (It.)
Silvester (L) forest
Sim (Heb.) obedient
    Simeon
Simon (Heb.) heard
    Simeon, Si
Simson—Simon's son
    Simpson
Sinclair (L) illustrious, St. Claire
Sing (Hindi) lion
Siran (Fr., Gk.) master
Sired (Teut.) conquering impulse
    Siri (Scand.)
Skegg (Scand., Teut.) beard
Slavomil (Slav.) glorious friend
Slavomir (Slav.) glorious peace
Sloan (Celt.) warrior
Socorro (Sp. from L) one who gives aid
Sohrab (Persian) ancient hero
Sol (L) sun, short Solomon
Solomon (Heb.) peaceful
    Sol, Suleiman, Shlomo, Salamon, Salamone

Solve (Scand., Teut.) healing warrior
Solveig (Scand., Teut.) healing drink
Son (Navajo Indian) star
Sophocles (Gk.) wise fame
Sophron (Gk.) of sound mind
Soroush (Persian) happiness
Sotero (Sp. from Gk.) savior
Soto (Blackfoot Indian) rain
Soud (Arab.) black
Spencer (OE) provisions keeper
Spiridion (Gk.) round basket
    Spiridon, Spyro
Srijan (Hindi) good man
Stacy (L) firmly established
Stafford (OE) landing ford
Standish (OE) stony park
Stanfield (OE) stony field
Stanford (OE) stony ford
Stanhope (OE) stony hollow
Stanislaus (Slav.) glory of the camp
    Stanislas, Stas
Stanley (OE) stony meadow, var. Stanislaus
Stannes (Ger., Slav.) glory of the camp
    Stanislaus (Ger.); Stanislav (Pol.)
Stanton (OE) stone quarry
Stasny (Slav.) happy
Stedman (A-S) farmstead
Stefan (Ger.) Stephen
Sten (Teut.) stone
Stephen (Gk.) crown
    Etienne (Fr.); Stefano, Estevan, Esteban (Sp.);
    Stepan (Slav.); Stefanos (Gk.); Stefano (It.); Steffert, Stephan, Steven, Steve
Sterling (OE) honest value
Stewart (A-S) steward
    Stuart
Stigand (Teut.) mounting
Stillman (A-S) quiet
Stiwell (A-S) still spring

Stoddard (OE) horse keeper
Sükrü (Turk.) gratitude
Suleiman (Arab.) peaceful
Summer (OFr.) summoner
Sunil (Hindi) lotus; (Thai) onyx
Sutton (OE) south village
Sven (Scand.) youth
    Svend, Svens
Svenbjorn (Scand.) young bear
Sviatoslav (Russ.) holy glory
Swain (Teut.) youth
Syed (Arab.) gentleman
Sylvester—var. Silvan
Syvert (Scand.) conquering guard

T

Taber (Arab., Sp.) drummer; (OF) herald
    Tab
Taddeo (Aramaic) praise
    Tadeo (Sp.); Thady (Irish); Tahddej (Russ.);
    Thaddeus
Tade (Teut.) people's ruler
Tago (Sp. from Teut.) day
    Tajo
Ta'ib (Arab.) good
Tait (Scand.) cheerful
Tal (Heb.) rain, dew
Talbot (OFr.) bloodhound
Talhah (Arab.) acacia tree
Tamas (Hung.) Thomas
Tamerlane—conqueror
    Timor, Timur (Russ.)
Tamlane (Scot.) var. Thomas
    Tam

Tanguy (Celt., Fr.) warrior
Tatanka (Sioux Indian) black buffalo
Taye (Ethiopian) seen
Taylor (OFr.) tailor
Tayma (Arab.) good fortune
Teague (Celt.) poet
Tearle (OE) stern
Tebaldo (It. from Teut.) people's ruler
    Teobaldo (It.); Teobald (Pol.)
Tecle (Ethiopian) my plant
Ted (Teut.) rich guard, short Theodore
Tedman—short Theodmund; also short St. Edmond
Tedor (Ger.) Theodore
Teïlo (Fr., Gk.) people
Telford (Fr.) ironworker
Terence (L) tender
    Terry
Terrill (Teut.) martial ruler
Terriss—son of Terry
Terry (OE) people's rule; short Terence
Tertius (L) third
Tescelin (Fr.) var. Anselm
Thaddeus (Heb.) praised; (Gk.) gift of God
    Tad, Thad, Thadée (Fr.); Tadeusz (Pol.)
Thamar (Arab.) profit, song
Than (Burmese) million
Thanor (Arab.) song
Thatcher (OE) roofer
    Thaxter
Thayer (Teut.) nation's army
Theobald (Teut.) people's prince
    Teobaldo (It., Sp.); Tibalt (Basque); Thibaut
    (Fr.); Dietbold (Ger.); Theobaldo (Pol.)
Theodmund (Teut.) protector
Theodolf (Teut.) bold for the people
Theodore (Gk.) divine gift
    Teodorico (It.); Teodoro (Sp.); Todor (Basque);
    Feddor, Fyodor (Russ.); Tedor (Ger.); Teodor

(Pol.); Tudor (Welsh); Theodoric, Theodor, The-
odotos

Theophile (Fr. from Gk.) love God
Teofilo (It.); Gottlieb (Ger.); Theophilus

Theron (Fr. from Gk.) hunter, height

Thet She (Burmese) long life

Thias (Heb.) gift of God
Thiesli (Swiss)

Thibaud (Fr. from Teut.) people's prince
Tibaut, Thibault

Thierry (Fr. from Teut.) people's ruler
Tierri (Russ.)

Thieu (Fr. from Teut.) people's rule

Thomas (Aramaic, Heb.) twin
Tom, Tommy, Tam, Tamas (Hung.); Tamlane
(Scot.); Tomaso (It.)

Thor—Norse god of thunder
Thorbert, Thorold, Thorwald, Thurstan

Thorley (Teut.) Thor's meadow

Thornton (OE) thorn-tree farm

Thorold (OE) Thor's strength

Thorpe (Teut.) small village

Thurlow (OE) Thor's hill

Thurston (Scand.) Thor's stone

Tiago (Sp. from Heb.) supplanter

Tiberio (It.) of the Tiber
Tibère (Fr.)

Tibor (Slav.) holy place

Tiernan (Celt.) kingly

Tilden (OE) fertile valley

Tilford (OE) fertile ford

Timon (Gk.) honor

Timothy (Gk.) honors god
Timoteo (It.); Timothée (Fr.); Timotij (Pol.);
Timofei (Russ.); Tim

Tino—dim. Constantine

Titus (L) honored
Tito (Sp.)

Tobias (Heb.) God is good
  Toby, Tobi, Tobin; Tobia (It., Russ.); Tobias (Hung.); Tobiasz (Pol.); Tobeis (Swiss); Tobias (Sp.)
Toland (A-S) taxed land
Tollo (L) victor
Tolman (OE) tax collector
Tomaso (It.) Thomas
Tonatiuh (Aztec Indian) sun
Torbert (Teut.) Thor's brightness, glorious as Thor
Torchel (Teut.) Thor's cauldron
  Torkel, Torquil (Dan.)
Torin (Gaelic, Irish) chief
Torrance (Irish) var. Terrence
Toussaint (Fr.) all saints
Towfiq (Arab.) success
Townsend (OE) end of town
Trahern (Celt.) stronger than iron
Travers (OE) crossroad
  Travis
Tremayne (Celt.) stone town
Trent—English river
Trevor (Celt.) prudent
Trinidad (Sp. from L) trinity
  Trini
Tristan (Fr., Ger. from L) sad, hero in medieval romance
  Tristam
Truman (OE) loyal
Tryg (Nord., Teut.) true
  Trygve
Tudor (Welsh) Theodore
Tugay (Turk.) brigade
Tugrul (Turk.) Sultan's seal
Tulio (Sp. from L) lively
Tullus (L) title, rank, legendary king of Rome
  Tully
Tunstal (Teut.) Thor's wolf
Tunstan (Teut.) Thor's stone

Turan (Turk.) Central Asian tribe
Turner (L) lathe worker; (OFr.) champion
Tuwma (Arab.) Thomas
Tyler (OE) brickmaker
Tyrone (L) young soldier; var. Thor

U

Ugo (It.) Hugh
Uland (Teut.) noble land
Ulbrecht (Ger.) noble splendor
Ullric (Ger.) noble ruler, ruler of all
    Ulric, Ulrich; Ulrico (It.); Ulrique (Fr.)
Ulmer—var. Ulric
Ulysses (Gk.) angry, hero of *Odyssey*
    Uliseo (It.)
Üner (Turk.) famous
Upton (A-S) high town
Urban (L) of the town
    Urbain (Fr.); Urbano (It., Sp.); Urvan (Russ.)
Uriah (Heb.) Lord is my light
Urian (Gk.) heaven
Ursan (L) bear
Uzziel (Heb.) God is strong
    Uzziah

V

Vada (L) shallow place
Vadim (Slav.) dim. Vladimir
Vail (L) valley
    Vale
Val—short Valentine; (L) healthy; (Fr.) vail
    Valek (Ger.)
Valdemar (Fr., Ger.) famous power
    Valdemere, Valdemaro, (It., Sp.)
Valentin (Fr.) strong, brave
    Valentino, Valerio (It.); Valer (Ger.); Valentin,
    Valerij (Russ.); Valerien, Valens (Fr.); Valentyn
    (Pol.); Valya (Russ. dim.); Valentine, Val
Valerian (L) strong, brave
    Valery, Valerius
Valeska (Slav.) glory
Vali—Norse mythological figure
Van (Dut.) from
    Vander
Vance (OE) high place
Vandyke (Dut.) from the dike
Vanka (Russ.) dim. Ivan
VanNess (Dut.) headland
Vanni (It.) dim. Giovanni
Varden (Fr.) green hill
Varian (L) changeable
Varick (Teut.) protecting ruler
    Warrick
Varner—var. Warner, Werner, Vernon
Varney (Celt.) alder grove
Varuna—Hindu god of the heavens
Vasilij (Gk., Russ.) royal
    Vassia, Vasska—dim.

Vaughn (Celt.) small
Ved (Hindi) holy text
Vedie (L) see
Vedis (Scand., Teut.) sacred sprite
Veerpal (Hindi) brave one
Venn (OE) handsome
Vered (Heb.) rose
Verlon (L) spring
    Verlin, Verle
Vern (OE) alder tree; short Vernon
Vernal (L) spring
Vernier (Fr.) spring
Vernon (L) flourishing
Vesselin (Bulgarian) merry
Victor (L) conqueror
    Vittorio (It.); Victor (Sp.); Bitor (Basque); Viktor
    (Russ.); Victorien, Victorin (Fr.)
Vid (L) life
    Vida (Hung.)
Viho (Cheyenne Indian) chief
Vilen (Russ.) contraction V.I. Lenin
    Veelen
Vilibaldo (Port. from Teut.) resolute prince
Vincent (L) conqueror
    Vincenzo, Vincenzio (It.); Vicente (Sp.); Vincent,
    Vincien (Fr.); Vincens (Ger.); Vincente (Port.);
    Vince, Vin, Vinnie
Vinson—son of Vincent
Virgil (L) strong, flourishing
    Virgilio (Sp.); Vergil
Virode (Thai) light
Viron (L) spring
Vitale (It. from L) living
    Vital (Fr., Ger.); Vitalij, Vita (Russ.); Vitalis,
    Vitas, Vidal (Slav.)
Vito (It.) short Vittorio, Vitale; also var. Guido
Vladimir (Russ., Slav.) ruling world, possesses peace
    Vadim, Volodia, Wladimir, Vladislav
Vladislav (Russ.) possesses glory

Voiteh (Slav.) warrior
Volker (Ger.) people's guard
Volney (Teut.) of the people
Volodia (Slav.) dim. Vladimir
Vyvyan (L) lively
    Vivian, Vivien (Fr.); Bibiano (Sp.)

W

Wachiru (Kikuyu, Kenya) lawmaker's son
Wade (OE) wanderer
Wadsworth (OE) from Wade's estate
Wairia (Kikuyu, Kenya) milkman
Walbert (OE) bright power
Walbridge (OE) walled bridge
Walcott (OE) walled cottage
Waldemar (OE) ruler of the sea; (Teut.) mighty and
    famous
Walden (OE) woods; (Teut.) mighty
    Waldo, Waldon
Walder—var. Walter
Waldo (OE) ruler
    Waldron, Waldon
Waldrich (Teut.) powerful ruler
Walenty (Pol.) Valentin
Waleran (Teut.) healthy
Walford (OE) Welshman's ford
Walfrid (Ger.) peaceful ruler
Wali (Arab.) all-governing
Walker (OE) cloth worker, cleaner
Wallace (A-S, OFr.) stranger; (Teut.) Welshman
    Walsh, Wallis, Wally
Walter (Teut.) powerful warrior
    Gauthier (Fr.); Galtero (It., Sp.); Gualtiero (It.);
    Wat, Walt, Walder, Valter

Walton (OE) walled farm
Warand (Teut.) protecting
Ward (OE) guard
Ware (A-S) prudent
Warfield (OE) field dam
Warford (OE) ford by the dam
Waring (L) true
Warner (Teut.) protecting warrior, guard
    Warren, Varin, Werner (Ger.)
Warren (OE) preserve; (Teut.) protecting friend, game
    warden
Warrick (OE) village hero; (Teut.) protecting ruler
    Warwick
Warton (OE) tree farm
Wasfi (Arab.) my description
Washington (OE) place name
Wassif (Arab.) describer
Watkins (Celt.) ford
Watson—son of Walter
Wayland (OE) land near a road
Wayman (OE) sailor
    Wyman
Wang'ombe (Kikuyu, Kenya) owner of cows
Wanjohi (Kikuyu, Kenya) brewer
Warner (Teut.) guard
Wayne (OE) meadow, wagon maker
    Duane, Dwayne
Webster (OE) weaver
    Webb
Welby (OE) village near willow tree; (Scand.) farm by
    the spring
Weldon (OE) spring by the hill
Welford (OE) spring by the ford
Wellington (A-S) prosperous estate
Wells (OE) spring, well
Wendel (Teut.) wandering
    Wendelin (Ger.)
Wendell (Teut.) wanderer
Werner (Ger.) Warner

Wesley (OE) west meadow
   Westley
Weston (OE) west village
Weylin (Celt.) son of wolf
Whitby (Scand.) white settlement
Whitelaw (OE) white hill
Whitford (OE) white ford
Wilbur (A-S) beloved stronghold
Wildon (OE) wooded hill
Wilford (OE) willow-tree ford
Wilfred (Teut.) resolute peace
   Wilfrid, Wilfried
Wilhelm (Ger.) William
Willard (Teut.) brave will
Willebald (Dut., Teut.) resolute prince
   Willibald, Willibahld, Villibahld (Ger.)
William (Teut.) resolute soldier
   Guillaume (Fr.,); Guillermo (Sp.); Guglielmo
   (It.); Wilhelm, Willem (Ger.); Gillen (Basque);
   Will, Willy, Willie, Bill, Billy, Billie, Guilmot,
   Guillen, Wilmot, Liam
Willimar (Ger.) resolute fame
Willis—son of William
   Wilson
Wilmer (Teut.) beloved and famous
Wilmot (Teut.) resolute mood; var. William
Wilton (OE) farm by the spring
Windsor (Teut.) bend of the river
Winfield (OE) field
Winfred (Teut.) friend of peace
Winifrid (Celt.) white stream
Winslow (OE) friendly hill
Winston (OE) friendly farm
   Winton
Winthrop (OE) friendly village
Witram (Ger.) forest river
Wolcott (OE) wolf's cottage
Wolf (Teut.) wolf
Wolfgang (Ger.) wolf's progress

Woodrow (OE) hedgerow by the forest
Woodward (OE) forester
Worthington (A-S) riverside
Wright (A-S) worker
Wylie (A-S) beguiling
Wyman (A-S) warrior
Wyndham (OE) windy village
Wynne (Celt.) white, fair
Wytt (OFr.) guide

X

Xabat (Basque) Salvatore
Xarles (Basque) Charles
Xavier (Sp. from Basque) new house
    Javier
Xerxes—Persian king
Ximen (Sp.) obedient
    Ximon, Ximun (Basque)

Y

Yago (Sp.) Jacob, James
    Iago
Yahuwda (Arab.) praise God
Yahya (Arab.) living
Yana (Cherokee Indian) bear
Yann—var. John
Yao (Ewe tribe, Ghana) Thursday's child
Yardan (Arab.) king, merciful
Yarin (Heb.) understand

Yasir (Arab.) easy, soft
  Yasar
Yates (OE) gate
Yavuz (Turk.) bold, energetic
Yaw (Ashanti tribe, Ghana) Thursday's child
Yedidyah (Heb.) God loves
Yehiel (Heb.) God lives, may God live
  Jehiel, Yechiel
Yehudi (Heb.) praise the Lord
Yerahmiel (Heb.) God is merciful
Yestin (Welsh) just
Yigal (Heb.) redeem
Yitzhak (Heb.) Isaac
Yo (Burmese) honesty
Yonah—var. Jonah
York (Celt.) yew tree
Youri (Russ.) George
Yovel (Heb.) rejoicing
Yushua (Arab.) Joshua
Yves (Fr., Scand.) archer; var. Ivo

Z

Zacarias (Sp.) Zachariah
Zachariah (Heb.) remembered by the Lord, Jah is renowned
  Zachary, Zach, Zack, Zaquero, Zacarias
Zadornin (Basque) Saturnin
Zahid (Arab.) pious
Zahir (Arab.) evident, splendid
Zakariya (Arab.) God has remembered
Zayit (Heb.) olive
Zayn (Arab.) beauty, ornament
Zebadiah (Heb.) gift of the Lord
Zebulun (Heb.) exalt

Zekediah (Heb.) God is just
Zeno (Gk.) Zeus
Zenon (Gk.) from Zeus, stranger
Zibiah (Arab.) deer
Zimraan (Arab.) celebrated
Zion (Heb.) fortress
Ziv (Heb.) brightness
Zohar (Heb.) brilliance
Zoltan (Fr., Gk., Hung.) life
Zuhair (Arab.) little flower
Zu-wang (Chinese) grandfather's wish

FEMALE NAMES

A

Aanor (Fr.) var. Eleanor
Abay (Ethiopian) name for Nile River
Abbey (Heb.) source of joy; var. Abigail
    Abbe, Abby, Abbie
Abelia (Fr.) fem. Abel
    Abella
Abellona (Dan.) fem. Apollo
Abena (Ashanti tribe, Ghana) Tuesday's child
Abeni (Nigeria) we asked for her and she came
Abeque (Ojibway Indian) she stays at home
Abetzi (Omaha Indian) yellow leaf
Abey (Omaha Indian) leaf
Abeytu (Omaha Indian) green leaf
Abia (Arab.) great
Abida (Arab.) worshiper; (Heb.) my father knows, my
    God knows
Abigail (Heb.) source of joy
    Abbe, Abbey, Abby, Abbie
Abijah (Heb.) God is my father
    Abisha
Abla (Ewe tribe, Ghana) Tuesday's child
Ablah (Arab.) perfect, sister
Abra (Heb.) fem. Abraham; (Arab.) example, lesson
    Abrahana (Sp.); Abarrane (Basque)
Abrihet (Ethiopian) light, brightened
Acacia (Gk.) name of tree, symbol of immortality

Accalia (L) foster mother of Romulus and Remus, founders of Rome

Aceline (Fr. from Teut.) fem. Acelin (noble)
    Asceline

Acenith—African goddess of love

Achsah (Heb.) anklet

Acima (Heb.) the Lord will judge; fem. Acim, Achim

Ada (Ger.) prosperous, happy

Adah (Heb.) adornment

Adalee—combination Ada and Lee; also var. Adelaide

Adalia (Heb.) God is my refuge; (Teut.) var. Adelaide

Adaline—var. Adelaide

Adamina (Scot.) fem. Adam

Adamma (Nigerian) beautiful child

Adara (Gk.) beauty; (Arab.) virgin

Addula (Teut.) noble cheer

Addy (Teut.) awesome
    Adda, Addie; short Adelaide, Adeline

Ade (Fr., Ger.) noble
    Adde, Ado

Adela (OGer.) noble, of good cheer
    Adèle (Fr.); Addala, Adeliz, Adelais, Adella (Sp.)

Adelaide (OGer.) noble, kind
    Adeline (Fr.); Adelina, Adelaida (Sp.)

Adele (Fr., Ger.) noble
    Adeline, Adelaide, Adella, Adeau

Adelheid (Ger.) noble, kind
    Adela, Adelle, Della, Edeline, Heidi

Adelia—var. Adelaide, Adele

Adelicia (L, Teut.) noble cheer
    Adelice (Fr.)

Adelinda (Fr. from Teut.) noble, sweet
    Adelinde

Adena (Heb.) adornment
    Adene, Adina, Dena, Dina

Adeola (Nigeria) crown
    Dola (nickname)

Aderes (Heb.) covering, crown
    Aderet
Adi (Heb.) my adornment
Adiba (Arab.) cultured
Adie (Heb.) ornament
Adiella (Heb.) ornament of the Lord
Adila (Arab.) equal, like
Adilah (Arab.) honest
Adima (Teut.) noble, famous
Adin (Heb.) delicate, decorative
Adira (Heb.) noble, mighty; fem. Adir
Aditi (Hindi) free
Adiva (Arab.) pleasant, gentle; fem. Adiv
Adlai (Arab., Heb.) just
Adnette (Fr. from OGer.) noble
Adoncia (Sp.) sweet
Adonia—fem. Adonis
Adora (L) adored
Adoración (Sp.) adoration
Adra (Arab.) virgin
Adranuch (Thai) lady
Adria—var. Adrian
    Adrea
Adrian (L) of the Adriatic
    Adrienne (Fr.); Adriana, Adriane
Adsila (Cherokee Indian) blossom
Adva (Aramaic) wave
Adwoa (Ashanti tribe, Ghana) Monday's child
Adzo (Ewe tribe, Ghana) Monday's child
Afaf (Arab.) chastity
Afework (Ethiopian) golden mouth
Affrica (Gaelic) pleasant
    Africa (Sp.); Apirka (Basque)
Afi (Ewe tribe, Ghana) Friday's child
Afra (Arab.) earth colored; (Heb.) young deer; (Teut.)
    peaceful ruler, also short Aphrodite
    Aphra
Afraima (Arab., Heb.) fruitful
Afua (Ashanti tribe, Ghana) Friday's child

Agalia (Gk.) brightness
Agapé (Fr. from Gk.) love
Agate (OFr.) semiprecious stone
Agatha (Gk.) good
  Agathe (Fr.); Agapet (Ger.); Agapit, Agafia,
  Agafon (Russ.); Agace, Agacia, Aggie, Agueda
  (Sp.); Agate (Basque)
Agnes (Gk.) gentle, pure
  Agnese (It.); Agneta (Swed.); Inessa (Russ.);
  Ines, Inez (Port., Sp.); Ynes, Nessa,
  Neysa (Sp.); Nesta, Agnola, Agna, Annais,
  Anneyce
Agnola (It.) angel; var. Agnes
Agrippa (L) born feet first
  Agrippine (Fr.); Agrafina (Russ.)
Ahava (Heb.) love
  Ahuva, Ahuda
Ahsan (Arab.) charity
  Ehsan, Ihsan
Ai (Japanese) love, indigo blue
Aida (Arab.) reward, present; (Fr., Sp.) help
Aiko (Japanese) little love, beloved
Aileen (Irish from Gk.) light; var. Helen
  Eileen, Ilene
Aili (Scot.) Alice, also short Alison
  Allie
Ailith (OE) experienced fighter
  Aldith
Ailsa (Scot.) Elsa
Aimée (Fr.) beloved
Aine (Celt.) joy
Airlea (Gk.) ethereal
  Airlia
Aisha (Arab.) living
  Ayisha
Aithne (Celt.) fire
  Aine, Ena, Ethne
Akasuki (Japanese) bright helper
Akilina (Russ. from L) eagle

Baby Names from Around the World

Akiva (Heb.) protect
  Kiva, Kivi, Kiba
Akosua (Ashanti tribe, Ghana) Sunday's child
Aku (Ewe tribe, Ghana) Wednesday's child
Akua (Ashanti tribe, Ghana) Wednesday's child
Alaia (Arab.) sublime
Alameda (Sp.) poplar grove
Alanna—fem. Alan
  Lana, Allena, Allene, Alane
Alarice—fem. Alaric
Alastair (Scot.) fem. Alexander
Alba (L) white; also pet Alberta
  Albine, Albane
Alberga (L) white; (OGer.) noble
  Alberge (Fr.)
Alberta (OGer.) fem. Albert
  Alberte, Albertine, Berte, Elbertine (Fr.); Albertina, Berta, Elberta, Elbertina (Sp.)
Albine (Fr., L) white
Alcestis (Gk.) Greek mythological figure, offered her life to save her husband's and was rescued
Alcina (Gk.) enchantress
  Alzina
Alda (It., OGer.) rich, old; (OE) antiquity; fem. Aldo, Aldus
  Alida, Alcda, Aldea, Aldina, Aldine, Aldabella (It., Sp.)
Aldara (Gk.) winged gift
Aldis (OE) experienced in battle
  Aldith, Ailith
Aldona (OGer.) old
Aldonza (Sp.) sweet, character in *Don Quixote*
Aldora (A-S) noble gift
Aleda (OGer.) antiquity
  Alida, Alda, Aldina, Aldona, Aldine, Aldyne
Aleen (Dut.) alone; var. Helen
  Alene, Aline
Aleeza (Heb.) joy
  Aliza, Alizah, Alitza, Aleezah

118

Alegria (Sp.) happiness
  Allegria
Alena (Russ.) var. Helen
Alène (Fr., L) winged
Aleph (Arab., Heb.) first letter of the alphabet; tall, slender; prince
  Alef, Alev, Alif
Aleshanee (Coos Indian) she plays all the time
Alethea (Gk.) truth
  Alethia, Alithea
Aletta (L) winged, birdlike
  Aleta, Alette (Fr.)
Alexandra (Gk.) fem. Alexander
  Alexandre, Alexandrine, Alexine, Alexis (Fr.); Alessandra (It.); Alejandro (Sp.); Alesandere (Basque); Alexandria, Alexa, Ali, Alexina, Aliki, Aleki, Allesanda, Sandra, Sondra, Sandy, Alessia, Alison, Alyson, Alastair, Alista
Alfreda—fem. Alfred
  Elfreda, Freda, Elva
Algiane (Fr.) fem. Algis
Ali—short Alexandra, Alice, Alison
Alice—var. Adelaide
  Alicia, Alisha, Alyce, Alecia, Alissa, Alyson, Allison, Alie, Ali, Alilki, Alicen, Alix, Alyse
Alida (OGer.) antiquity
  Aleda, Alyda, Alda, Aldona, Aldine, Aldyne
Alif—var. Aleph
Aliki—var. Alexis, Alice
Alima (Arab.) wise
Aline (Fr.) fem. Alin; var. Adeline
  Alina
Alinor—var. Eleanor
Aliosha—var. Adelaide
Alioth (Gk.) brightest star in Big Dipper handle
Alisha—var. Alice
Alison—var. Alice
Alissa—var. Alice
  Allissa, Alysa

Alita (Sp.) noble
Alix (Fr., Teut.) noble
    Alex, Alissandre, Lissandre
Aliya (Arab.) sublime, exalted; (Heb.) ascend
    Aliyah
Aliye (Arab.) noble; (Turk.) high, exalted
Aliza—var. Aleeza, Alice
Alkas (Coos Indian) she is timid
Allana—fem. Allan
Allegra (It.) happy
Allison—var. Alice, Alexander
    Alison, Alyson, Alisa, Lissa
Allyriane (Fr. from Gk.) lyre
Alma (L) fair, kind, loving; soul; (Arab.) learned;
    (Celt.) good; (Russ.) name of river; (Heb.) maid-
    en, girl
Almarine (OGer.) work ruler
    Almeria
Almeda (Celt., Fr.) princess; var. Maëlle
Almeta (L) ambitious
Almira (Arab.) princess, exalted; (Sp.) woman from
    Almeira
    Mira
Almodine (L) precious stone
Almudena (Sp.) name for Virgin Mary, Our Lady of
    Almudena
Alodie (A-S) wealthy, prosperous
Aloisia (It.) fem. Alosio
    Aloysia
Alona (Heb.) oak tree
    Allona, Allonia, Alonia
Alonsa (Sp.) Alonso
    Alonza (It.)
Aloysia (Ger.) fem. Aloysius
    Aloisia
Alpha—var. Aleph
Alphosine—fem. Alphonse
Alta (L) high
Altair (Arab.) bird

Althea (Gk.) wholesome; (L) healer
    Thea
Altheda (Gk.) flowerlike
Aluma (Heb.) girl
    Alma, Alumit
Alva (L) white
    Alva, Albine, Albina, Alvah
Alvar (Nord., OGer.) elf army
Alvina—fem. Alvin
    Alvinia, Vinia, Vina, Vinny
Alvita (L) vivacious
Alysia (Gk.) captivating
Ama (Ewe tribe, Ghana) Saturday's child
    Ami
Amabel (L) lovable, beautiful
    Mabel, Anabel, Annabella, Arabell, Arabella
Amada (L) beloved
Amadahy (Cherokee Indian) forest water
Amadée (Fr.) love God
Amadore (It.) gift of love
    Amadora
Amal (Arab.) hope
Amala (Arab.) hope
Amalia (Port., Slav. from Teut.) industrious; var.
    Amelia
    Amalie (Ger.); Amalina (It., Sp.); Amaline (Fr.);
    Amalija (Russ.)
Amalida (Teut.) industrious heroine
Amana (Heb.) faithful
Amanda (L) beloved, lovable
    Manda, Mandy, Amandine
Amany (Arab.) aspiration
Amapola (Arab.) flower
Amara (Gk.) immortal, unfading, steadfast; (Thai)
    eternal; also paradise in Abyssinian legend
    Mara, Amarinda (Gk.)
Amarantha (Gk.) immortal; flower name
    Amarante (Fr.); Amaranta (Sp.); Amarande
    (Basque)

Amariah (Heb.) God has spoken
Amaris (Heb.) God has promised
    Amariah
Amaryllis (Gk.) fresh, sparkling; flower name
Amata (L) beloved
    Amy, Ami, Amé, Aimée, Amada (Fr.)
Ambar (Hindi) sky
Amber (Arab.) semiprecious stone, believed to have
    healing power
Ambhom (Thai) sky
Ambrosine—fem. Ambrose
    Ambrosina, Ambrosia
Amde (Ethiopian) pillar
Ameerah (Arab.) princess
    Amira, Meerah, Mira
Amelia (L) industrious; persuasive
    Amalia (Port., Sp.); Amalie, Ameline, Amélie,
    Méline (Fr.); Emily, Millie, Milly, Amalina,
    Amelina
Amelinda—combination Amelia and Linda
Amenaide (Gk.) satisfied
Amera—var. Ameerah; also short America
    Mera
America (Sp.) fem. Amerigo
Amethyst (Gk.) precious stone
Ami (Fr.) var. Amy; (Heb.) my people; (Ewe tribe,
    Ghana) Saturday's child
    Amia (Heb.)
Amice—var. Amy
    Amecia
Amilia (L) affable
Amina (Arab.) secure, honest; (Heb.) honest
Aminta (Gk.) protector
Amira (Arab.) princess, cultivated; (Heb.) speech
Amisa (Heb.) friend
    Amissa
Amita (Heb.) truth
Amità (It.) friendship
Amma (Ashanti tribe, Ghana) Saturday's child

Amor (Sp.) love
  Maite (Basque)
Amorette (Fr.) little love
Amparo (Sp.) defense
Amy (OFr.) loved
  Aimée, Aimie, Ami, Amia, Amata, Amada,
  Esma, Esmé
Ana (Heb.) grace
  Anne (E., Fr.); Annabelle, Annemarie, Anne-
  Aymone, Annelle, Annette, Ninette, Nanette,
  Nanine, Nanice, Annice, Annise, Anaïs, Annick,
  Anouk, Anouche, Annaëlle (Fr.); Anne-
  lore, Anneliese (Fr., Ger.); Anna, Annabella,
  Anna Maria, Annamaria (It.); Ana, Ana Maria,
  Anita, Ninor, Nanor, Nina, Nita (Sp.); Nina
  Anya, Ania, Anka, Anyushka (Rus., Slav.);
  Anke, Anki, Anika (Dut.); Annabelle,
  Annimae (Scot.); Nancy, Netta, Nettia, Anona,
  Nan, Nanny
Anaïs (Fr.) var. Anne
Anamari (Basque) Ana Maria
Ananke (L, Gk.) goddess
Anastasia (Slav. from Gk.) resurrection
  Anastay, Stacey, Stacie; Anastase, Ana-
  staise (Fr.)
Anat (Heb.) sing
Anatola (Gk.) from the East
Ancelote (Fr.) fem. Lancelot
Andra (ONorse) breath; also var. Andrea
Andrea (Gk.) fem. Andrew
  Andrée (Fr.); Andreana (It.); Andreas (Ger.);
  Andresa (Sp.); Andere (Basque)
Andromache (Gk.) wife of Hector in *Iliad*
Anemone (Gk.) breath, nymph changed into a flower,
  flower name
Ange (Fr.) angel
  Angèle, Angeline, Angelique (Fr.); Angelina,
  Angela, (It., Sp.); Angelika (Ger.); Angeleta,
  Anjelika, Anjela, Angie

Annabel (Scot.) combination Anna and Bella
    Annabella
Anne-Aymone (Fr.) combination Anne and Anemone
Anneliese (Ger.) combination Anne and Lisa
Annelle—var. Ann
    Annell
Annissa (Arab.) charming, gracious
Annonciada (Sp.) var. Anunciación
    Annunziata (It.)
Annot (Heb., Scot.) light
Anonna (L) goddess of harvest
    Anona
Anselma (OGer.) fem. Anselm
    Anselme (Fr.)
Ansonia—fem. Anson
Anthea (Gk.) flowerlike
    Anthia
Anthemia (Gk.) blooming
Antonia (L) fem. Anthony
    Antonine, Antoinette (Fr.); Antonina, Antonia
    (It., Sp.); Antonetta, Netta, Nettie, Netty, Toni,
    Tonia, Toinette (Fr. var.)
Anunciación (Sp.) religious holiday of the annunciation
    of the Virgin Mary
    Deiene, Deikun, Deiña (Basque)
Anupa (Hindi) beautiful, good
Appolinia (Gk.) fem. Apollo
    Abbeline, Abbelina
April (L) when earth opens for growth of spring
Aqiyla (Arab.) precious, noble; fem. Aqiyl
Aquilina (Sp.) fem. Aquilino
Ara (Arab.) opinions; (Ger., L) eagle heroine, altar
    Arabella
Arabel (L) beautiful eagle, fair altar
    Arbell, Arbela, Orabelle
Arama (Basque) name for Virgin Mary
Araminta—combination Arabelle and Aminta
Arava (L) coast
    Aravellel, Arville

Arcadia (Sp. from L) adventurous woman
Arcelia (Sp. from L) treasure chest
Arda (Heb.) bronze
 Ardah, Ardath
Ardelia (L) zealous
 Ardia, Ardis
Ardelle (L) ardent, industrious
 Ardene, Ardine, Ardis, Ardelis, Ardella, Arda,
 Ardelia
Arden (L) eager, fervent
 Ardin, Ardena, Ardenia
Ardith (Ger.) prosperous; var. Edith
Ardra (L) var. Ardelle; (Celt.) noble, high
Arela (Heb.) angel
 Arella
Areta (Gk.) virtuous
 Areta, Arette, Aretina
Aretha (Gk.) nymph, orchid
 Arethusa, Oretha
Arezou (Persian) wishful
Argira (L) name for Juno, wife of Jupiter
Argyrea (Gk.) silvery
Ariadne (Gk.) very holy one, daughter of sun god
 Ariadna (Sp.); Arene (Basque); Arianna, Ariane
 (Fr.)
Ariana (Welsh) silvery
 Ariane (Ger.)
Arielle (Heb.) lion of God
 Ariela, Ariellel, Ariel
Arilda (Ger.) hearth, home
Ariminta (Heb.) lofty
Arion (Gk.) poetess; (Heb.) melodious
Arista (Gk.) the best
Arlana (Celt.) pledge; fem. Arlen
Arlene (OGer.) girl; fem. Arlen
 Arlena, Arleen, Arline, Arlina, Arlynn, Arla,
 Arly, Arlette, Arlana
Arlise (Heb.) pledge; fem. Arliss
 Arlyss

Armelle (Fr. from Celt.) princess
Armilla (Ger.) bracelet
Armine (Fr.) fem. Armand
    Armantine
Armineh (Persian) desire, goal; fem. Arman
Arna (Heb.) cedar
    Arnit
Arnalda (Sp.) fem. Arnald
Arona—fem. Aaron
Arrosa (Basque) Rose
Artemisia (Gk., Sp.) perfect
Arvada (Dan.) eagle
Asa (Japanese) morning
Asceline (Fr.) fem. Ascelin
Asención (Sp.) Ascension of Christ into Heaven
Ashira (Heb.) wealthy
Ashley (OE) from ash-tree meadow
Asima (Arab.) protector
Asisa (Heb.) ripe
Aspasia (Gk.) lily, welcome, winning
Asphodel (Gk.) lily
Asta (Gk.) star; (L) venerable; short Augusta
    Étoile, Esther (Fr.); Hadassah (Heb.); Estella
    (It.), Stella, Estrella (Sp.)
    Astera, Asteria, Astra, Hester
Astra (Gk.) star; Astrea, goddess of justice returned to
    heaven after stay on earth and became constella-
    tion Virgo
Astrid (Norse) divine strength; var. Astra
Asunción (Sp.) feast of the Assumption, August 15
    (reception of Virgin Mary into Heaven)
Asvoria (Nord., Teut.) divine prudence; fem. Asvor
Atalia (Heb.) the Lord is mighty, also queen of Judah
    Atalaya (Sp.)
Atara (Heb.) crown
Atepa (Choctow Indian) wigwam
Ateret (Heb.) crown
Athalia (Heb.) the Lord is mighty
Athanasia (Gk.) immortal; fem. Athanasius

Athena (Gk.) goddess of wisdom
    Athène (Fr.)
Athor—Egyptian goddess of beauty
Atia (Arab.) old
Atifa (Arab.) affection, sympathy, benevolence
Atira (Heb.) prayer
Atiya (Arab.) gift
Attila (Gk.) fem. Attilio
Atura (Heb.) crowned
Atzimba—native princess of Mexico
Au (Japanese) meeting
Auda (OFr.) old, rich
    Aude
Audra—var. Audrey
Audrey (OE) noble strength
    Audra, Audie, Audre
Audris (OGer.) fortunate
Augusta (L) venerable
    Augustine, Austine (Fr.); Augustina, Austina, Tina, Gussie
Aura (Gk.) soft air, breeze; (L) gold
    Aure (Fr.)
Aurelia (Sp. from L) gold
    Aurelie (Fr.); Aureliana, Aurita (Sp.); Aurelne (Basque); Aurea, Aural, Aurel, Orelia, Orel, Orelee
Aurora (Fr. from L) dawn, Roman goddess of the dawn
    Aurore (Fr.) Ora, Rora, Rory, Zora, Zorica (Slav.)
Ava (Ger.) bird; var. Avis and Eve
Avalon (Fr., L) island
Ave (L) hail
Avel (Heb.) breath
Aveline (Heb.) pleasant; (OFr.) nut
    Avelaine
Avi (Heb.) father
Avice (Fr.) var. Hedrige
    Arcicia, Havoise
Avirit (Heb.) air

Avital (Heb.) father of dew
Aviva—fem. Aviv
    Avivi, Avivit
Awenasa (Cherokee Indian) my home
Awinita (Cherokee Indian) young deer
Awusi (Ewe tribe, Ghana) Sunday's child
Axelle (Fr.) fem. Axel
Ayako (Japanese) damask pattern
Ayala (Heb.) deer
Ayamé (Japanese) iris flower
Ayao (Ewe tribe, Ghana) Thursday's child
Ayashe (Ojibway Indian) little one
Ayesha (Persian) happy
Ayita (Cherokee Indian) first in the dance
Aza (Arab.) comfort
Azalea—flower name
    Azalia
Azami (Japanese) thistle flower
Azar (Persian) flame
Aziza (Heb.) fem. Aziz
Azora (Persian) sky blue

B

Babette (Fr.) dim. Barbara, Elisabeth
Badriyah (Arab.) full moon
Balbine (Fr. from L) stammerer
Balere (Basque) Valery
Baptista (Gk.) baptizer; fem. Baptiste
    Battista, Bautista, Baptiste (Fr., It., Sp.)
Baraka (Arab.) white one
Barbara (Gk., L) the stranger
    Basha (Pol. dim.)
Barnesse (OFr.) baroness
    Barnessa

Barrie—fem. Barry
Bashiyra (Arab.) joy
Basile—fem. Basil
    Basilia, Basille (Fr.)
Basima (Arab.) smiling
Bathilda (Ger.) heroine, bold
    Bathilde, Bertilde (Fr.)
Bathsheba (Heb.) daughter of Sheba, daughter of the
    oath, pledge
    Bathseva, Bathshua, Batshua, Batsheba, Bat-
    sheva, Sheba, Bethsabée (Fr.)
Bathshira (Arab.) seventh daughter
Batia (Fr.) dim. Bathilde
Beata (L) blessed
Beatrice (It., L) she blesses or makes happy
    Beatrix, Beatrisa, Bebe, Trix, Trixy, Trixie, Bee,
    Bea
Bebba (Swiss from Heb.) God's oath
Becky—short Rebecca
Bee—nickname Beatrice, now also used as separate
    name
Bée (Fr.) dim. Benedicte
Behira (Heb.) brilliant
Bela (Slav.) white
Belda (Fr.) beautiful lady
Belinda (It.) symbol wisdom and immortality; (Sp.)
    combination Bella and Linda (pretty)
Beline (Fr., OGer.) goddess
Belisama—Roman divinity like Minerva, goddess of
    wisdom, skill and invention
Belita (Sp. from L) beautiful
Bella (L) beautiful; dim. Isabella
    Belle, Bell, Bellette (Fr.)
Bellona (L) war goddess
Bema (Gk.) fair speech
Bena (Heb.) wise; fem. Ben
    Béna (Fr.)
Benedetta (It. from L) blessed; fem. Benedict

Bénédicte (Fr.); Benita (Sp.); Benedicta, Benetta, Benita

Benigna (It., Sp.) kind, blessed

Benita (It., Sp.) blessed

Bera (Nord., Teut.) bear

Berdine (Ger.) bright maiden

Berna—short Bernadine

Bernadette (Fr.) fem. Bernard

Bernardine (Fr.) fem. Bernard
Bernardina

Berneta—var. Bernadette
Bernetta, Bernette

Bernice (Gk.) brings victory
Berenice

Bertha (Ger.) bright, glorious; fem. Albert
Berthe (Fr.); Berta (Sp.)

Bertilde (Teut.) heroine

Bertina (Ger.) bright, shining; fem. dim. Albert, Bertram, Herbert, Hubert

Berura (Heb.) pure

Beryl (Gk.) sea-green gem; (Heb.) precious stone; (OGer., Yiddish dim.) bear

Bess—dim. Elizabeth

Beth (Heb.) house; dim. Elizabeth

Bethany (Heb.) house of God

Bethel (Heb.) house of God
Bethuel, Bethune (Scot.)

Bethesda (Heb.) house of mercy, name of pool in Jerusalem having healing waters after an angel stirred it

Bethiah (Heb.) daughter of Jehovah, worshiper of Jehovah
Beia, Betia

Betsy—dim. Elizabeth

Bettina (Heb.) dim. Elizabeth
Bettine

Betty—dim. Elizabeth
Bette, Bett

Beulah (Heb.) bride
    Beula
Beverly (OE) from beaver meadow
Bianca (It.) white
Bibiana (Sp.) var. Vivian
    Bibiane (Fr.)
Bienvenida (Sp.) welcome
Billie—fem. William
Bina—dim. Sabina
Birjis (Arab.) planet Jupiter
Birkita (Basque) Brigitte
Bithron (Heb.) daughter of melody
Blair (Celt.) from the plain
    Blaire (Fr.)
Blaise (Fr.) stammerer
    Blaize, Blaze
Blanche (Fr.) white, fair
    Blanca (Sp.); Zuria (Basque)
Blanchefleur (Fr.) white flower
Blanda (L) seductive, flattering, caressing
    Blandina, Blandine
Blenda (Ger.) glorious, dazzling; (Swed.)
    heroine
Bliss (A-S) joy
Blossom (OE) bloom
Blythe (A-S) glad, joyous
Bodgana (Pol.) God's gift
    Bohdana
Bona (Heb.) builder; (L) good
Bonfilia (It.) good daughter
Bonita (Sp.) pretty
Bonne (Fr.) good
Bonnibel (L) good and beautiful
    Bonnibelle (Fr.); Bonny, Bonnie
Bonnie (L) sweet and beautiful; dim. Barbara
Brandy—fem. Brandon
Brenda (Norse) fem. Brand
Brenna (Celt.) dark hair

Bretta (Celt.) from Britain
Bret, Brit, Brite, Brittany, Brita
Briana (Celt.) strong; fem. Brian
Brice (A-S) nobleman; (Celt.) quick
Bryce
Bride (Celt., Scot.) strength
Briget, Bridget, Brietta (Irish); Brigida (It.);
Birgit, Birget, Brigitta (Swed.); Brigitte (Fr.);
Brites (Port.); Britte, Brita, Brigid, Biddy
Bridget (Irish) strong, lofty
Brie (Fr.) region in France
Bree, Briet
Brilliana—daughter of the English governor of Brill, in
Holland, in seventeenth century
Brina (Celt., Slav.) protector; fem. Brian
Brit (Celt.) speckled
Brita (Ger.) var. Bridget
Bronislava (Slav.) fem. Bronislav
Brooke (OE) stream
Bruna (It., Russ., Teut.) dark, brown; fem. Bruno
Brunhilda (OGer.) heroine, Norse mythological figure
Brunhilde, Brinhilde, Hilda, Hildi

C

Cacilia (Ger.) var. Cecilia
Cacilie
Caitlin (Welsh) var. Catherine
Cala (Arab.) castle
Calandra (Gk.) lark
Calandre (Fr.); Calandria (Sp.)
Calantha (Gk.) beautiful blossom
Calida (Gk.) most beautiful; (L) loving, ardent
Calli, Calla
Calista (Gk.) most beautiful
Calliste, Caliste (Fr.); Cally

Calla (Gk.) beautiful; flower name (lily)
Callia (Fr., Gk.) Calliope
Callidora (Gk.) gift of beauty
Calligenia (Gk.) daughter of beauty
Calliope (Gk.) beautiful voice
Callis (L) cup
Calvina—fem. Calvin
Calypso (Gk.) sea nymph in *Odyssey,* orchid, conceal
Camelai—flower name
Camilla (L) freeborn, attendant at ceremony
    Camille (Fr.); Cama, Cammy
Candace (Gk.) glittering, glowing white
    Candice, Candis, Candy, Candie
Candida (It., L) white
    Candide (Fr.); Candy
Candra (L) moon, luminescent
Cantara (Arab.) small bridge
Capucine (Fr.) cape
Cara (It., L) dear; (Celt.) friend
    Carina, Carine, Karina, Karine, Carrie, Carry,
    Carabelle
Caren—var. Catherine
    Carin, Caryn, Caron, Karen, Karin, Karine
Cari (Turk.) flowing like water
Carilla—fem. Charles
Carina (L) keel, dear; var. Catherine
    Karina, Caren, Carin, Karen, Caryn, Carine
    (Scand., Sp.)
Carisa (L) artful
Carita (L) charity
Carla—fem. Charles
    Carlita, Carly, Carrie, Karla
Carlin—var. Caroline, Charlotte
    Carleen, Carlyn, Carly, Cailen, Carlyne (Fr.)
Carmel (Heb.) vineyard, garden, Mt. Carmel
    Carmella, Carmine, Carmelina (It.); Carmelita
    (Sp.)
Carmen (L, Sp.) song
    Carminia

Carmiel (Heb.) garden of the Lord
Carnation—flower name; (L) incarnation
Carol (Fr.) song of joy; fem. Charles
  Carole
Caroline—fem. Charles
  Carolina, Caroleen, Carolyn, Caroly,
  Carrie
Casilda (L) home
Cass—short Cassandra
Cassandra (Gk.) prophetess, helper of man
  Cass, Cassie
Cassia (Gk.) cinnamon
Castelia (Gk., Sp.) purity, crystal clear waters
  Casta
Catalina (Sp.) Catherine
Cathelle (Fr.) var. Catherine
Catia (Fr.) dim. Catherine
Cecile (L) gray eyes, blind
  Cecilie, Cecilia, Ceciliane
Celena (Gk.) daughter of mythological figure, Atlas
  Selena
Celeste (L) heavenly
  Celestia, Celestine, Celina, Celinda, Celia
Celine (Fr.) fem. Marcel dim. Marcéline
Cenobia (Sp.) Zenobia
Cesarina (Sp.) fem. Cesar
  Césarine, Césarie (Fr.); Cesárea (Sp.); Kesare
  (Basque)
Chaitra (Hindi) zodiac sign Aries
Chanda (Sanskrit) great goddess
Chandra (Sanskrit) outshines the stars
Chantal (Fr.) song, stone, God grants
Chao-xing (Chinese) morning star
Chapa (Sioux Indian) beaver
Charis (Gk.) love, charity, grace
Charissa (Gk.) love
Charity (L) charity
  Charité (Fr.); Carita, Charis, Charissa, Charita,
  Carissa

Charlene—fem. Charles
  Charlena
Charlotte (Fr.) fem. Charles
  Carlotta (It., Sp.), Charla, Charlene, Charlaine
  (Fr.); Lotta, Lola, Lottie, Carla, Carleen, Carlota,
  Carly, Charla, Charleen, Charlotta, Charmain,
  Charmion, Charo, Charyl, Karla, Karlene, Kar-
  lotta, Loleta, Lolita, Lotte, Sharleen, Sharyl,
  Sherry, Sheryl
Charmaine (Fr. from L) song
  Charmain
Charmeme (Gk.) rejoicing the spirit; source of joy,
  charm
Charmian (Gk.) joy
Charo (Sp.) var. Caroline, Charlotte
Chastity (L) chastity
Chava (Heb.) life
  Hava
Chaya (Heb.) life; fem. Chaim, Haim
  Haya
Chela (Gk.) claw
Chelo—short Consuela
Chelsea (A-S) port
Cher (Fr.) dear
  Chere, Cheri, Cherie, Cherrie, Cheryl, Sheryl,
  Sheryll, Sherelle, Cherylie, Chery, Cheret
Chéron (Fr.) beloved
  Caron, Chérot, Chéret
Cheryl—var. Charlotte, Cher
Chiara (It. from L) famous, light
Chika (Japanese) near, thousand rejoicings
Chinyelu (Ibo tribe, Nigeria) gift of God
Chiquin (Sp.) dim. Concepción
Chita (Sp.) dim. Concepción
  Conchita
Chitose (Japanese) thousand years (wish for longevity)
Chiyo (Japanese) thousand generations
Chizu (Japanese) thousand storks
Chloe (Gk.) blooming

Chloris (Gk.) pale
Cho (Japanese) butterfly; long life
Cholena (Delaware Indian) bird
Christa (Fr.) var. Christine
Christabel—combination Christa and Belle
  Christabelle
Christel (Scot.) Christine
  Christelle (Fr.); Kristel, Christabel, Christabelle
Christiane (Fr.) fem. Christian
  Christiana, Christie, Christine, Chris, Chrissi,
  Christa, Kristen, Kristine, Kristina, Krista (Ger.,
  Scand.); Kit, Christel, Christelle, Kristell (Fr.);
  Cristina (Sp.); Christina, Chrystal
Christine (Fr. from L) Christian
Chryseis (Gk.) chrysanthemum, golden hair, character
  in *Iliad*
  Chrysilla
Chrystal (L) clear, jewel name; var. Christine
  Crystal
Chumani (Sioux Indian) dewdrops
Cindy (Gk.) dim. Cynthia
Cinnie (Celt., Fr.) beauty
Claire (Fr., L) bright, clear
  Clara, Clarissa (Sp.); Clarisse, Clarice, Clara (It.);
  Clarinda, Clarine, Clarita, Clareta, Cliarra, Clari,
  Clarette; Kalarc, Garbi (Basque)
Clarimond (OGer., L) bright protection
Clarinda—combination Clara and Florinda
Claude (Fr. from L) lame
Claudette (Fr.) dim. Claude
Claudia (It.) fem. Claudio
Claudine (Fr.) var. Claude
Cleanthe (Gk.) glorious flower
Clelia (L) glorious
Clementina (Sp. from L) gentle, merciful
Clementine (Fr.) fem. Clement
Cleopatra (Gk.) glory of the father, queen of Egypt
Clérisse (Fr.) var. Claire
  Clarisse, Clarice

Clio (Gk.) celebrate, one of nine Muses, history
Clorinda (Sp, from Persian) famous
Cloris (Gk.) goddess of flowers
Clotilda (OGer.) heroine; fem. Clovis
    Clotilde (Fr.); Clautilda (Sp.)
Coleen (Gaelic) girl
Colette (Fr.) dim. Nicolette, fem. Nicolas
    Coleta (Sp.); Kolete (Basque)
Coline (Fr.) fem. dim. Nicolas
    Nicoline
Columbine (L) dovelike, flower name
Concepción (Sp.) immaculate conception
    Concetta (It.); Concha, Conchita (Sp.)
Concheta (It., Sp.) dim. Concepción
Conrada (Sp.) fem. Conrad
    Coradinna
Consolación (Sp.) consolation
Consolata (Sp.) var. Consuela, Consolación
Constance (L) constant
    Constancia (Port.); Constanta, Constantia, Con-
    stantina, Constanza (It., Sp.)
Consuelo (Sp.) consolation
    Consuela, Chelo
Cora (Gk.) maiden
    Corine, Corrine (Fr.); Corina (It.); Corey
Coral (Heb.) small pebble
Coralie (Fr.) coral
    Coralee
Corazon (Sp.) heart
Cordelia (Celt.) jewel of the sea
Coretta—nickname Cora
    Corette
Corey (Gaelic) ravine
Corliss (OE) cheerful
Cornelia (L) horn; fem. Cornelius
    Cornélie (Fr.)
Corvina (L) ravenlike
Cosima (Gk.) order, universe; fem. Cosmo
    Cosme (Sp.); Kosma (Basque)

Couronne (Fr.) crown
Courtney (L) court
  Courtland
Cressida—medieval legendary figure of *Troilus and Cressida*
Crissann—combination Christine and Ann
Cyanea (Gk.) sea blue
Cybele (Gk.) nature goddess of ancient Asia Minor
Cyma (Gk.) flourish
  Syma
Cymo (Gk.) sea foam
Cynthia (Gk.) name for Artemis, goddess of the moon
  Cindy
Cyprien (Fr.) Cypriot
  Cyprienne, Sabria
Cyra (Gk.) ruler; fem. Cyrus
Cyrilla (L) fem. Cyril
  Cirilla

D

Dacy (Fr.) from Acy, in France
Dagania (Heb.) ceremonial grain
  Daganya
Dagmar (Nord., Teut.) Dane's joy, brightness
Dahab (Arab.) gold
Dahlia—flower named after Swedish botanist, Dahl
Dai (Japanese) great
Daisy—flower name
Dale (ONorse) valley
Dalice—var. Dalit
Dalida (Fr.) var. Adelaide
  Dalidou
Dalila (Sp.) Delilah

Dalit (Heb.) draw water
    Dalis
Dalmace (Fr. from L) from Dalmatia
    Dalmas, Dalmassa, Dalma
Damara (Gk.) gentle girl
    Damaris, Maris, Mara, Mari
Damaris (Gk.) calf; var. Damara
Damia (Gk.) goddess of forces of nature
Damien (Fr.) patron saint of surgeons
    Damia, Damian, Damiane, Damiana
Dana (Heb.) fem. Dan; (Celt.) from Denmark; (Gk.)
    mythological figure, mother of Perseus
Danaé (Fr.) var. Danielle
Danay (OFr.) Dane, Danish
    Dané, Danet
Danella—var. Daniella
Dani (Heb.) my judge
Danica (Slav.) morning star
Danielle (Fr. from Heb.) fem. Daniel
    Daniela (Sp.); Danita (It., Sp.); Danele (Basque);
    Danitza (Slav.); Danila, Danelle, Danella,
    Danette, Dani, Danie, Dany, Danya, Danice,
    Daniss
Dara (Heb.) heart of wisdom, compassion
    Darya, Daria
Daralis (OE) beloved
    Daralice
Darcy (Irish, OFr.) from Arcy; (Gaelic) dark
Daria (Sp.) fem. Darius; (L) give
    Darya, Darice, Dari
Darian (Persian) wealthy; (A-S) dear
    Darien, Dorian, Doriane, Darrell, Daryll
Darlene (OE) dim. Daralis
Dasha (Russ.) gift of God
Davida (Heb.) fem. David
    Davina, Davita, Davi, Daviane, Davinia
Dawn (OE) dawn
Day (OE) day

Dayle (OE) valley
    Dale
Dea (L) goddess
Deanna—var. Diane
    Deane, Dee, Deanne
Deborah (Heb.) bee
    Debora, Devorah
Decia (L) tenth
    Decima
Dee—short Deanna, Deanne
Deifilia (It., Sp. from L) daughter of God
Deirdre (Celt.) causes fear; (Irish) young girl
    Derdre
Dela—short Adela
Dela O Kande (Nigerian) first daughter born after many
    sons
Delia (Gk.) from Delos; name for Artemis, goddess of
    the moon
Delicia (Sp.) delightful
Delilah (Heb.) delicate
Della—short Adelle; combination Delia and Belle
Delma (Sp.) of the sea
Delmira—var. Edelmira
Delphine (Fr., Gk.) flower name, dolphin; fem. Dau-
    phin
    Delfin (Sp.); Delbin (Basque); Delfine
Delta—nickname Odele
Demetria (L) var. Demeter, Roman goddess of the
    Earth
Den (Japanese) bequest from ancestors, tradition
Denise (Fr.) fem. Denis
    Denice, Denyse
Derede (Gk.) gift of God
Derora (Heb.) brook
Désirée (Fr.) desire, much-wanted child
    Desideria (Sp.); Désir, Désirat (Fr.)
Desta (Ethiopian) happiness
Detta—short Benedetta, Henrietta

Deva (Hindi) divine, moon goddess
    Cama-Deva
Devi (Hindi) resides in Heaven
Devona (OE) from Devon
Devora (Heb.) var. Debora
Diana (L) goddess of the moon, hunting
    Diane, Dayana, Deanna, Deanne, Dee, Di
Didi (Heb.) beloved
Didiane (Fr.) fem. Didier
Didière (Fr.) fem. Didier
Didilia (Slav.) fertility goddess
Dido—queen of Carthage
Didrika—fem. Dieterich
Dielle (Fr.) worshipper of God; (L) goddess
    Diella
Digna (Sp. from L) worthy
    Dinya
Dina (Heb.) judged; (Fr.) dim. Dominique
    Dinah
Dinorah (Aramaic) light
Dionne (Gk.) mythological figure, daughter of Heaven
    and Earth; mother of Aphrodite
    Dione, Dionis, Diona, Dioné (Fr.)
Dirce (Gk.) mythological figure, queen of Thebes
Dita—dim. Edith
Divya (Hindi) divine, heavenly
    Divia
Dixie (Fr.) ten, name for the South
Dodie (Heb.) beloved
Doli (Navajo Indian) bluebird
Dolly—nickname Dorothy
Dolores (Sp.) sorrows, reference to Maria de los Do-
    lores, Virgin Mary
Dominica (Fr.) Lord
Dominique (Fr.) Lord
Domitiane (Fr.) Lord
    Domitia
Donata (Basque, It., Sp. from L) gift

Donelle—combination Dona and Ella

Donna (L) lady

Donoma (Omaha Indian) visible sun

Dora (Gk.) gift; var. Doris; short Dorothea

Dorcas (Gk.) gazelle

Dorée (Fr.) var. Dorothy

Doreen (Irish) dim. Dora, Theodora; (Celt.) moody, (Fr.) golden
> Dorine (Fr.)

Dorella—dim. Dora; combination Dora and Elle

Doretta (L) gift of God

Dorian (Gk.) ancient Greek people of Doris; var. Darian; (L) golden; var. Theodora; combination Dora and Ann
> Doriane

Doris (Gk.) region of ancient Greece, home of the Dorians; Doric girl

Dorleta (Basque) name for Virgin Mary

Dorothy (L) gift of God
> Dorothée (Fr.), Dorotea (Sp.); Dorote (Basque); Doretta, Dorinda, Dodie, Dot, Dotty, Dottie

Douce (Fr.) sweet

Drew (Gk.) vision; (OGer.) carrier; (OFr.) sturdy; (Welsh) wise; dim. Andrew
> Dru

Dru (Teut.) skilful; short Drusilla

Drusilla (L) strong
> Druscilla, Drucilla

Duana (Gaelic) song

Dulce (Sp.) sweet
> Dulcie

Dulcinea (Sp.) sweet, character in *Don Quixote*

Durga (Hindi) mythological figure, wife of Siva

E

Eartha (OGer.) earth
Ebba (Fr., OGer.) strong
    Ebbane
Eberta (Teut.) brilliant
Echo (Gk.) sound
Eda (A-S) happy
Edana (Celt.) ardent, flame; fem. Edan
Edda (Scand.) mythological figure
Edeline (Fr., OGer.) noble, of good cheer
    Adeline
Eden (Heb.) delightful
Edina (A-S) prospering, noble
Edith (Teut.) rich gift; (A-S) prospering
    Editha, Edita, Edithe, Edythe
Edmonda (A-S) fem. Edmond
    Edmée, Edma (Fr.)
Edna (Heb.) rejuvenation
Edra (Heb.) mighty; (Teut.) prosperous
    Edrea
Edris (A-S) fem. Edric
Edwige (Fr. from OGer.) happy combat
Edwina (OE) fem. Edwin
    Edina
Efua (Ewe tribe, Ghana) Friday's child
Eglantine (OFr.) sweetbrier, wild rose
Eimile (Irish) Emily
Eithne (Gk.) little fire
    Ethne, Aithne
Elaine (Gk.) light
Elais (Gk.) olive tree
Elata (L) exalted

Elberta (Teut.) brilliant
Elda—short Edlyn; (A-S) princess; (It.) var. Hilda
Eldora (Sp.) golden
  Eldoris
Eldrida—fem. Eldred
  Aldrida
Eleanor (Gk.) light
  Eléonore, Aliénor, Hélène, Enora (Fr.); Eleanora
  (It.); Eleanore, Helen, Ellen, Elen, Eileen (Irish);
  Elena (Sp.); Lena, Elna, Elnora, Lienor, Nora,
  Norina, Nonnie, Nell, Nelly, Nellie, Aileen,
  Alena, Alene, Helena, Lorle
Electra (Gk.) bright; amber hair
Elefteria (Gk.) freedom
Eleuteria (Gk.) freedom, daughter of Jupiter and Juno
Elfrida (Teut.) wise, strong
Elga (Teut.) holy; (OE) noble
  Olga, Helga, Elgiva
Elia—fem. Elias
Eliane (Fr.) fem. Elias
  Eline, Eliette, Elyette
Elice (Heb.) fem. Elias
Elidi (Gk.) gift of the sun
Eliora (Heb.) God is my light
  Eleora
Elisa (Basque) Elizabeth
Elisée (Fr.) var. Elisabeth
  Elise, Lise, Lison, Elizé, Elissa, Liese
Elisheva (Heb.) God is my oath
  Elisheba
Elita (OFr.) chosen
Eliza (Heb.) consecrated to God
Elizabeth (Heb.) consecrated to God
  Elisa, Elissa, Eliza, Elsbeth, Elspeth (Scot.); Elsa-
  beth, Elsie, Beth, Bettina, Betsy, Bess, Libby,
  Lizzie, Liz, Lison, Lise, Liese, Ilse, Ilsa, Isa,
  Elisea, Else; Elizaveta (Russ.); Isabel (Sp.);
  Elisabeth (Fr.); Elisabet
Elkana (Heb.) God has acquired

Ella (A-S) elfin, all; (Heb.) Lord
    Ellina, Elletta, Elladine
Ellamae—combination Ella and Mae
    Ellamay
Ellen (Gk.) light
    Elena, Elenita (Sp.); Eléna (Fr.)
Ellice (Heb.) fem. Elias
Elma (Gk.) amiable; combination Elizabeth and Mary
Elmina (Teut.) famous
Elmira (OE) noble, famous
Elna (Gk.) light; var. Helen
Elodie (L) white blossom; var. Alodie
Eloine (L) worthy to be chosen
Eloise (Teut.) famous in battle; var. Louise
Elora (Gk.) light
Elsa—var. Elizabeth
Elsie (OGer.) noble; var. Alice; short Elizabeth
    Elsa, Else, Ilse, Ilsa, Ilyse, Elyse
Elva (A-S) elfin
Elvera (L) fair
Elvia (Sp.) yellow
Elvina (OE) elf friend
Elvira (Sp.) white, fair; (OGer.) elf rule
    Elvire (Fr.)
Elvita (L) life
Elyse—var. Elsa, Elsie
Embla—in Scandinavian mythology, first woman
Emelda (Sp.) var. Emily
    Emilia, Emelia, Amalia, Amelia, Emera, Emeline
Emeline—(L, Teut.) var. Emily; (L) faultless
Emerald (OFr.) precious green stone
Émeraude (Fr.) emerald
Emerence (L) deserving
    Émérentienne (Fr.); Emerentia (Ger.)
Émérika (Fr.,OGer.) mistress of the house
Emilie (Fr. from L, Teut.) industrious
    Emilianne, Emilienne (Fr.); Emilienna, Emilia,
    Emiliana (Sp.); Milia (Basque); Meliosha (Slav.)
Emily (L, Teut.) industrious

Emma (Teut.) grandmother
    Emmélie (Fr.); Emmy, Irma, Erma, Emmylou
Emmanuelle (Fr.) fem. Emanuel
Emmeranne (Fr., OGer.) raven
Ena (Gk.) praise; (Celt.) fire; var. Anne
Encarnación (Sp.) incarnation, reference to Christian
    mystery of the word into flesh
    Gizane (Basque)
Endora (Fr., OGer.) noble
Engracia (Sp.) graceful
Enid (Celt.) spirit, soul, purity; (Welsh) woodlark;
    (A-S) fair
Ennata (Fr., Gk.) goddess
Enona (Gk.) nymph on Mt. Ida, married Paris
Enora (Fr., Gk.) light
Ephratah (Heb.) fruitful
    Afrata, Erda, Ertha
Erena—var. Irene
Erendira (Sp.) Mexican princess, she smiles
Erianthe (Gk.) sweet as many flowers
Erica (Teut.) powerful, regal, flower; fem. Eric
    Erika
Erin (Gaelic) peace, name for Ireland
Erina (Gaelic) girl from Ireland
Ermelinde (Fr., OGer.) honor, sweetness
Erna (OE) bird, eagle; (Teut.) short Ernestine
Ernestine—fem. Ernest
    Ernesta, Erna
Errita (Basque) Rita
Esi (Ewe tribe, Ghana) Sunday's child
Esmé (A-S) gracious protector; (Fr.) var. Amy; fem.
    Esmond; short Esmeralda
Esmeralda (Gk.) emerald; (L) brilliant
    Émeraude (Fr.)
Espérance (Fr.) hope
    Esperanza (Sp.); Espe (Basque)
Esseline—(Fr.) var. Asceline
    Aseline, Eslyn
Estefania (Sp.) fem. Stephen

Esther (Gk., Heb., L) star
    Ester, Hester; Estelle, Étoile (Fr.); Estella (It.);
    Estrella (Sp.); Astrid (Nord.); Estra, Astra, Asta,
    Essie
Estelle (Fr.) star
    Estelon
Esteva (Sp.) fem. var. Stephen
Estra (A-S) goddess of spring; var. Esther
Estrella (Sp.) star
    Estela, Ester; Izarra (Basque)
Etain (Irish) shining
Ethel (Heb.) noble
Ethelda (Teut.) noble, wise
    Ethelind
Étienne (Fr.) fem. Stephen
Étoile (Fr.) star
Etsu (Japanese) delight
Etta (OGer.) little; dim. Henrietta
Eudine (Fr., OGer.) noble
Eudora (Gk.) beautiful gift, Greek goddess
Eudosia (Gk.) esteemed
    Eudocia
Eugenia (Gk.) wellborn, noble
    Eugénie, Genia, Génie (Fr.); Evedni, Evguesha,
    Guesha, Ghenia (Slav.)
Eulalia (Gk.) speaks sweetly, well-spoken
    Eulalie (Fr.); Eula, Yula
Eunice (Gk.) good victory
Euphémie (Fr., Gk.) well-known
Euphrasia (Gk.) joyous
    Euphrosyne, Euphrasie (Fr.); Euphrosine
Eurielle (Celt., Fr.) angel
Eurydice (Gk.) mythological figure, wife of Orpheus;
    great justice
    Euridice
Eusébie (Fr., Gk.) pious
Eustacia—fem. Eustace
Euveline—var. Eveline, Eve
Eva (Heb.) life

Eve, Eveline, Hava, Chava, Chaya, Haya (Heb.);
Evita (Sp.); Evka (Slav.)

Evadne (Gk.) mythological figure, water nymph; sweet
singer; var. Eve
Evadine, Ariadne

Evalinde (Ger.) var. Eva; combination Eva and Linda

Evangeline (Gk.) brings good news, gospel

Evania (Gk.) tranquil

Evanthe (Gk.) flower

Eve (Heb.) life
Evain, Evin, Evan, Eveline, Euveline, Evelaine,
Evette, Evelina, Eveleen, Evelyn, Avelin, Lena,
Lina

Evelyn—var. Eve

Everilde (Fr. from OGer.) honor in battle

Exaltación (Sp.) reference to Holy Cross
Gorane (Basque)

F

Fabia (It., Sp.) fem. Fabio
Fabienne (Fr.); Fabiana (It., Sp.);
Fabiola (Fr., It., Sp.)

Fabrienne (Fr.) fem. Fabron

Fadilla (Fr.) dim. Françoise

Fadiyla (Arab.) plentiful, superiority, knowledge

Fadwa (Arab.) self-sacrifice

Faida (Arab.) abundant

Fairoue (Arab.) turquoise, precious stone

Faith (L) trust, faith
Fé (Sp.); Fay, Faye

Fakhri (Arab.) my pride

Fala (Choctaw Indian) crow

Fanchon—fem. Francis

Fanette (Fr.) dim. Stephanie

Fania (Teut.) free
    Fanny
Fanny—dim. Stephanie, Françoise
Fantine (Fr.) childlike
Farah (Arab.) happiness; (Persian) happiness, name of
    former Queen of Iran
Faramond (OGer.) journey protection
    Fara
Farasat (Arab.) keen eye
Farhanna (Arab.) joyful
Farhat (Arab.) joy
Farica (Teut.) peaceful rule
Farida (Arab.) unique; precious gem
Farideh (Persian) glorious
Fariha (Arab.) happy
Faten (Arab.) fascinating, charming
Fathia (Arab.) my conquest
Fatima (Arab.) weaning, daughter of Mohammed;
    (Port.) Our Lady of Fatima, name for Virgin Mary
Faunia (OFr.) young deer
Fausta (It., Sp.) fortunate
    Fauste, Faustine (Fr.); Faustina (Sp.)
Fay (OFr.) fairy; dim. Faith
    Faye, Fae
Fayre (OE) beautiful
Fe (Sp.) faith
Fedora (Gk.) divine gift
Felda (Teut.) field
Felicia (L) happy; fem. Felix
    Felicie, Félicité, Félicienne (Fr.); Felicidad,
    Felisa (Sp.); Felicie, Felicity, Feliz, Felise, Felita
Fenella (Celt.) white shoulder; var. Elena
Feodora (Russ.) fem. Theodore
Feride (Turk.) unique
Feriga (It., Teut.) peaceful ruler
Fern (Gk.) feather, fern; short Fernanda
Fernanda—fem. Ferdinand
    Fernande (Fr.)
Ferola (L) iron

Fidelia (It. from L) faithful
Fidèle (Fr.)
Fidelity (L) faithfulness
Fifi (Fr.) dim. Josephine
Fifine
Filiz (Turk.) shoot or tendril of vine
Fina (Sp.) short Josefina
Fiona (Celt.) white, fair; var. Sophie
Flaminia (Fr., It. from L) Roman priest
Flavia (L) blonde, yellow
Flavie, Flavière (Fr.)
Fleda (Teut.) swift
Fleta
Fleur (Fr.) flower
Fleurette
Flor (Sp.) flower
Flora
Flora (L) flower
Florence, Florette (Fr.); Florencia, Florida (Sp.);
Fiorenza (It.); Florella, Floria, Floris, Florica,
Flori, Lore (Basque)
Florence (L) flowering
Floriane (Fr.) flowering
Forouzeh (Persian) happy, turquoise
Fortuna (It. from L) goddess of good luck
Fortune
Franca (L) the Franks
France (Fr.) France, Frances
Frances (Teut.) free
Françoise (Fr.); Francesca (It.); Francisca (Sp.);
Fran, Franny, Fanny
Françoise (Fr.) Frances
Franceline, Francette, France, Francique, Fan-
chon, Fadil, Francine
Frayne (OE) foreigner
Freda (Teut.) peaceful
Frida
Fredella—combination Fred and Ella

Freya (Scand.) mythological goddess of love, Wagnerian character

Fritzi (Ger.) fem. Fritz

Fronia (L) wisdom

Fulvia (L) blonde

Fuscienne (Fr. from L) black
Fusciane, Fescenia

G

Gabinia (Fr., It. from L) famous Roman family, name of city in central Italy
Gabia

Gabrielle (Fr. from Heb.) God is my strength
Gabriella, Gabriela (It.); Gavrila, Gavra (Slav.); Gabi, Gaby, Gabie

Gachui (Kikuyu, Kenya) chick

Gael (Celt.) strong

Gaëlle (Fr., Ger.) stranger, foreigner
Gaëlla

Gaëtane (Fr., It.) city in central Italy
Gaetana

Gaïa (Fr., Gk.) the Earth
Gaya, Gaïane, Gayana

Gail, (OE) lively
Gale, Gael

Gala (Sp. from L) from Gaul

Galane (Fr.) flower name
Galliane

Galatea (Gk.) white
Galatée (Fr.)

Galia (Heb.) God has redeemed; (Teut.) stranger, foreigner; (L) Gaul; (Fr.) var. Galane
Gallia, Galliane, Galya

Galiena (OGer.) lofty
Galilahi (Cherokee Indian) amiable, attractive
Gallia (Fr.) Gaul
    Gala, Galla
Gallienne (Fr. from Teut.) stranger
Garabi (Basque) Clara
Garda (Teut.) guarded
Garthe (ONorse) garden, enclosure
Gavra (Slav.) Gabrielle
    Gavrila
Gay (Fr.) merry
    Gai
Gedalia (Heb.) God is great
Gefania (Heb.) vineyard of the Lord
Gelasia (Gk.) laughing
Gellia (Fr.) var. Galane
    Gelliane
Gelsomina (It.) Jasmine
Gemma (Fr., It., Sp.) precious stone
    Gema, Gemmie
Gen (Japanese) source, spring, fountain
Geneva (OFr.) juniper; var. Geneviève
    Genevra (It.); Genoveva (Sp.); Gena, Ginevra,
    Ginebra
Geneviève (Fr. from Celt.) white wave, white as foam
    Genoveva (Sp.); Geva, Gina
Georgette (Fr.) fem. George
    Georgia, Georgiana, Georgina, Georgine, Geor-
    geta, Inoulia
Geraldine—fem. Gerald
    Geralda, Giralda (It., Sp.)
Gerda (Ger.) guarded, protected
Gerde (Ger.) fighter
Germaine (Fr.) German, protector
    Germana, Ghermana, Germinie
Gertrude (Teut.) fighter
    Gertie, Trudy, Trude, Gerta
Gervaise (Fr. from Teut.) war eagerness
    Gerva

Baby Names from Around the World

Ghada (Arab.) young, fresh, tender
Ghaliyah (Arab.) musk perfume
Ghauaala (Arab.) gazelle
Ghislaine (Fr. from OGer.) sweet pledge
    Guilaine
Ghita (It.) pearl; short Margarita
Giacinta (Gk., It.) purple, flower name
Gilberte (Fr., Ger.) fem. Gilbert
    Gilberta
Gilda (Celt.) servant of God; (OE) gilded; var. Hilda
    Gildas, Kermeilde (Basque)
Gilia (Fr.) flower name
Gillian (L) youth
Gillie (Fr.) fem. Gilles
Gin (Japanese) silver
Gina (It.) var. Eugenia; short Geneviève
    Luigina
Ginditta (It. from Heb.) praise
    Ginda
Ginebra (Sp. from Celt.) white as foam; (Fr.) dim.
    Genviève
    Ginessa (Sp.); Ginette (Fr.)
Ginevra (It. from Celt.) white as foam
Gisèle (Teut.) pledge
    Gisela
Gita (Hindi) song
    Guita, Ghita
Giula (It. from L) youth
    Giuliana, Giulietta
Gladys (L) lame; (Welsh) Claude; (Celt.) rich
    Gladez, Glawdys
Glen (Gaelic) valley
    Glenna, Glennis, Glynis
Gloria (L) glorious
    Gloriana, Gloriane
Gloriana (L) queen in Spenser's *Faerie Queene*; var. Gloria; combination Gloria and Ana (Sp.)
Glynis (Gaelic) valley

Godva (Teut.) divine gift
Golde (Teut.) golden hair
    Golda
Golnar (Persian) center of flame, red flower
Gonça (Turk.) flower bud
    Goncha, Concha
Grace (L) graceful
    Gracia (Sp.); Grazia (It.); Gracie, Graciane, Gra-
    tiane, Gracienne, Gracieuse (Fr.); Grata, Gratia,
    Graciana, Engracia (Sp.); Griselda (Ger. var.)
Grania (Celt.) love
Graziella (It. from L) thanks, grace
Gredel (Gk.) pearl
    Gretel, Gretal, Gretchen
Gregoria (Fr.) fem. Gregory
    Gregoria (Sp.)
Greta (Swed.) short Margareta
Griselda (Teut.) stone, heroine, patience, gray eyes;
    var. Grace
    Griseldis, Grizelle
Gryta (Gk.) pearl
Guadalupe (Sp.) valley of the wolf; name for Virgin
    Mary, reference to Our Lady of Guadalupe
    Lupe, Lupita, Pita (Sp.); Godalupe (Basque)
Guan-yin (Chinese) goddess of mercy in mythology
Guda (Ger., Scand.) divine
Gudny (Ger., Scand.) divine freshness
Gudrid (Ger., Scand.) divine impulse
Gudrun (Ger., Scand.) divine wisdom
    Gudruna
Guennola (Celt.) white
Guia (Sp.) fem. Guy
Guinevere (Celt.) fair lady
    Guenevere, Gwenovere, Guenievre
Guiomar (Ger.) famous in battle
Guity (Persian) world
Guri (Hindi) goddess of abundance
Gustava—fem. Gustave
Gustel (L) exalted; (Ger.) short Augusta

Gutki (Pol., Yiddish) dim. good
Gwen (Welsh) white; (Celt.) fair; short Gwendolyn, Gwenevere
    Gwenna
Gwendolyn (Celt.) white brow
    Gwendolin, Gwendolen, Gwendoline, Gwennoline
Gweneth (Celt.) fair; (Welsh) blessed
    Gwyn, Gwyneth
Gwny (Welsh) blessed

H

Haala (Arab.) glory
Habiba (Arab.) beloved
Hada (Sp.) destiny
Hadar (Heb.) ornament
Hadiyah (Arab.) guide to righteousness
Hafiza (Arab.) guardian
Hagar (Heb.) flight
Haide (Gk., Sp.) modest
    Haidée, Aidee, Haidee, Heidi, Haydee
Hajar (Arab.) wandered
Hajira (Arab.) wandered
Haldis (Teut.) stone spirit
Haley (ONorse) heroine; (A-S) holy, healthy; fem. Hal
    Hally, Hallie, Halette
Halima (Arab.) kind, humane
Halime (Turk.) mild, gentle, docile
Haloke (Navajo Indian) salmon
Hama (Japanese) shore
Hana (Arab.) joy, satisfaction; (Japanese) blossom
Hanaan (Arab.) mercy
Hanako (Japanese) flower, fair blossom
Hannah (Heb.) grace, prayer; var. Ana

Hannat (Arab.) grace
Haralda (Teut.) mighty in battle; fem. Harald
    Harelda
Harmonie (Fr. from Gk.) harmony; Greek mythologi-
    cal figure, daughter of Mars and Venus
Harriet (Teut.) mistress of the home
    Harriette, Harrietta, Hatty, Hattie
Harué (Japanese) springtime bay
Haruko (Japanese) tranquil, spring
Hasiyna (Arab.) beautiful
    Hacenah
Hasna (Arab.) beautiful
Hati (Swiss) pure
Hatsu (Japanese) first-born
Hauwa (Arab.) living, name for Eve
Haya (Japanese) quick, light, nimble
Hayfa (Arab.) slender
Hazar (Arab.) nightingale
Hazeka (Fr., OGer.) rabbit
Hazel—flower name
Heather (OE) heather
Hebe (Gk.) youth
Hecuba (Gk.) wife of Priam in *Iliad*
Heda (Ger.) war
    Hedy
Hedda (Ger.) var. Hedgwig; (Teut.) refuge in battle
Hedia (Gk.) pleasing
    Hedyla
Hela (Scand.) goddess of shadow
Helen (Gk.) light
    Helene, Helinie, Helaine (Fr.); Helena, Elena,
    Heliena, Helenka, Lana (Slav.); Elena (Sp.); Nell,
    Nellie, Nelly, Leni, Nelliana, Ileana, Elna, Elane,
    Elana
Helga (Scand. from Tuet.) holy
      Olga, Elga
Helia (Gk.) sun
Heloise (Fr.) Louise

Helsa (Dan.) dim. Elizabeth
Henrietta (Ger.) mistress of the home
    Henriette (Fr.); Enriqueta (Sp.); Henrika (Swed.)
Hepsiba (Heb.) my delight is in her
Hera (Gk.) goddess Juno, queen of gods, goddess of
    womanhood and maternity
Hermandine—fem. Hermes
    Herma, Hermine
Hermia—short Hermione
Hermione—daughter of Venus and Mars
    Herminia (Sp.); Irmina (Basque); Armonia, Har-
    monia
Hernanda—fem. Hernando
Hertha (Ger.) earth
Hesper (Gk.) evening star
Hester (Persian) star; var. Esther
    Hestia
Hetty (Persian) star; short Henrietta, Hester
Hibah (Arab.) gift
Hida (Ger., Sp.) warrior
    Gilda, Heidi, Hilde
Hidé (Japanese) excellent, fruitful, superior
Hidéyo (Japanese) superior generations
Hilary (L) cheerful
    Hillary
Hilda (Teut.) warrior
Hildegard (Teut.) protection in battle
Hiro (Japanese) broad
Hiroko (Japanese) magnanimous
Hisano (Japanese) long plain
Hmwe (Burmese) fragrant
Hodiya (Heb.) God is my splendor
Holly (OFr.) shrub
Honi (Heb.) gracious
Honor (L) honor
    Honora, Honorine, Honorata (Sp.)
Honovi (Hopi Indian) strong deer
Hope (OE) hope

Hortense (L) gardener
  Hortensia (Dut., Ger.); Hortense (Fr.); Ortensia (It.)
Hoshiko (Japanese) star
Huberta—fem. Hubert
Huette (Fr.) fem. Hugh
Hughette (Fr.) fem. Hugh
Hulda (Heb.) weasel
Hulweh (Arab.) sweet
Humayra (Arab.) reddish
Huriyah (Arab.) virgin of paradise
Hyacinth (Gk.) purple, flower name
  Jacinthe, Hyacinthe (Fr.); Giacinta (It.); Jacinta (Sp.); Hyacinthia, Hyana

I

Ianira (Gk.) enchantress
Ianna—fem. Ian
  Iane
Ianthe (Gk.) violet-colored flower, sea nymph
Ida (OE) protection; (Norse) labor; (Teut.) happy; (Gk.) mountain in Crete
  Idamay, Idalon, Idalea, Idelle, Idette, Idena, Idaïa, Idalie, Iba
Idalia (Sp. from Gk.) sunny
Idaline (Teut.) noble, happy
  Adalia, Adaline
Idane (Norse, OGer.) labor
Idelia (Gk., Sp.) noble
Idola (Gk.) vision
Idonna (Teut.) industrious
Idora—var. Isadora
Idra (Aramaic) fig tree

Ifeoma (Ibo tribe, Nigeria) beautiful girl, a very good thing (birth of daughter)

Ignacia—fem. Ignatius
  Ignatia

Iku (Japanese) nourishing

Ilana (Heb.) tree
  Ilanit

Ileana (Sp.) var. Elena
  Iliana, Ilona (Hung.)

Ilia (Heb., Russ.) God is the Lord

Ilit (Aramaic) best
  Ila

Ilithya (Gk.) goddess, protector of women in labor

Ilka (OE, Scot.) kind, sort; (Teut.) industrious

Ilona (Hung.) light

Ilse (Ger. from Heb.) God's oath; (Teut.) noble cheer

Iluminada (Sp.) illuminated

Ima (Heb.) mother
  Yma

Imelda (Celt., Fr.) princess

Imogene (L) image

Ina (L) mother; var. Agnes; originally dim. ending, then separate name

Indi (Hindi) Indian

India—var. Diana
  Indiana

Iné (Japanese) rice

Ines (Sp.) Agnes
  Inez

Inessa (Russ.) Ines

Inga (Scand., Slav., Teut.) daughter; (OE) meadow
  Inge, Inger

Ingrid (Scand., Teut.) daughter; var. Inga; fem. Ing, Norse mythological god of fertility

Inmaculada (Sp.) Immaculate Conception
  Sorkunde (Basque)

Inocencia (Sp.) innocence
  Inocenta, Innokenta

Io (Gk.) daughter of river god, so beautiful Jupiter fell
in love with her
Iona (Gk.) violet, purple jewel
Ione, Ionia, Ioessa
Iordana (Slav.) Jordan
Iphigenia—Greek mythological figure
Iphigénie (Fr.)
Irene (Gk.) peace
Irina (Russ.); Irena, Erena, Eirene, Ira, Iraïs,
Rena, Rina, Reni, Rini, Rina
Iris (Gk.) rainbow, messenger of the gods
Irma (L) noble; short Hermione; (OGer.) war god
Irmina, Erma
Irune (Basque) trinity
Isa (Teut.) iron; (Sp.) var. Elisa, Luisa
Isabel (Sp.) Elizabeth
Isobel (Scot.); Isabelle (Fr.); Isabela, Isabella,
Bella (It.); Belle, Bell
Isadora—gift of Isis, Egyptian goddess
Isidora, Dora, Idora
Isamu (Japanese) vigorous, robust
Isaura (Gk.) soft air
Aura, Isaure
Iseline (Fr.) var. Isabelle
Iseult (Celt.) fair, heroine of legend of Tristan and
Isolde; (OGer.) ice rule
Isolde, Yseult, Isolda
Ishi (Japanese) stone
Isi (Choctaw Indian) deer
Isis—Egyptian goddess, symbol of life and fertility
Isleen—var. Eileen
Ismelda—var. Imelda
Ismene (Gk.) sister of Antigone; var. Imelda
Isolde (Celt.) fair; (OGer.) ice rule
Isolda (Sp.); Yseult (Fr.)
Isra (Thai) freedom
Istiyr (Arab.) Esther
Ita (Celt.) thirsty

Ito (Japanese) thread
Itta (Fr., Ger.) work
Iva—fem. John
    Ivana (Russ.)
Ivria (Heb.) original name of the Jews
    Ivriah
Ivrit (Heb.) Hebrew language
Ivy (OE) plant name
Iwa (Japanese) rock
Izella (Ger.) little princess
    Isella

J

Jacinta (Sp.) hyacinth; (Gk.) purple, flower name
    Jacinth, Jacinthe, Hyacinth, Hyacinthe (Fr.); Gia-
    cinta (It.); Jakinda (Basque)
Jacoba—fem. Jacob
Jacqueline (Fr.) fem. Jacques
    Jacquelyn, Jacquenette, Jacquette, Jacquine, Ja-
    cotte, Jacquemine, Jacquine (Fr.); Jacklin, Jack-
    lyn, Jackie, Jacky, Jakeza
Jada (Fr., Sp.) green stone
Jaen (Heb.) ostrich
Jaffa (Heb.) beautiful
    Jafit
Jagoda (Slav.) strawberry
Jahara (Arab.) jewel
Jakinda (Basque) hyacinth
Jala (Arab.) clarity
Jaleh (Persian) rain
Jalena—combination James and Ellen or Lena, Jane
    and Ellen
    Jalene
Jalila (Arab.) great

Jamila (Arab.) elegant, beautiful
Jan—var. Jane; short Janette
Jana—with Janus, presided over day and night
Jane (Heb.) gracious; fem. John
    Janel, Janelle, Janet, Janette, Janella, Janie,
    Janna, Janita, Janina, Janine, Jean, Jeannie, Janie,
    Janee, Jehane, Jana, Janis, Janice, Jovanna, Juana,
    Juanita (Sp.); Giovanna (It.); Janita (Dut.); Jo-
    hanna, Johanne (Ger.); Sheena, Shena (Gaelic);
    Zaneta (Russ.); Janique, Jeanne, Johanne (Fr.)
Janine (Fr.) Jane
    Janina
Janis—var. Jane
    Janice
Jannan (Arab.) heart, soul
Jannat (Arab.) heaven, garden
January (L) January
    Janvier, Janvière (Fr.)
Jaouda (Arab.) goodness
Jara (Slav.) Gertrude
Jardena—fem. var. Jordan
Jarita—Hindu legendary bird
Jasmine (Persian) flower name
    Gelsomina (It.); Gelsomine (Fr.); Yasmin, Yas-
    mine, Yasmina, Jasmina, Jessamine
Jeanne (Fr. from Heb.) grace of God
    Jeannice, Jeannine, Jemmie
Jehanne (Fr., Heb.) grace of God
Jemima (Arab.) dove
    Yomina (Heb.); Jonina
Jennifer (Celt.) white wave; var. Jeanne
    Jenny
Jerina—fem. var. Gregory
Jerusha (Heb.) inheritance
Jessamine (OFr.) jasmine
Jessica (Heb.) grace of God
Jessie (Heb.) God's grace
    Jesse, Jess

Jesusa (Sp.) fem. Jesus
Jethra—fem. Jethro
Jetta (L) coal black
Jewel (L) jewel, joy
    Joia, Joya (Sp.)
Jezabel—var. Elizabeth
Jill—var. Gillian
Jillian—var. Gillian, Juliana
Jimena (Sp.) fem. var. Simeon
Jin (Japanese) tenderness, humanity, excellence
Jing-wei (Chinese) small bird; daughter of sun god in
    mythology
Joanne—var. Jeanne
Joaquina (Sp.) fem. Joaquin
    Joaquine
Jobina (Heb.) fem. Job
Jocasta (Gk.) mythological figure, wife and mother of
    Oedipus
Jocelin (Fr., Heb.) fem. Jacob; (L) beautiful
    Joceline, Jocelyn, Jocelyne, Joslin, Josline
Jocheved (Heb.) God is glorious
    Jochebed
Jodelle (Fr.) fem. var. Joel
Jodi—var. Judah
    Jodie, Jody
Joelle (Fr.) fem. Joel
    Joela, Joella, Joelliane
Joia (L) merry
Jolanta—var. Yolanda
Jolie (Fr.) pretty, merry
Joliette (Fr.) violet
    Joletta
Jona—fem. Jonah, John
Jonati (Heb.) my dove
Jordan (Heb.) descendant; var. Georgiane
    Jordane (Fr.); Jordana (Sp.); Yordana (Basque)
Jorina—fem. var. Gregory
Josanne—combination Joseph and Anne

Joscelin (L) just
    Joscelind
Josée (Fr.) fem. Joseph
    Josepha, Josapha, Josèphe (Fr.); Yosebe (Basque)
Josephine (Heb.) fem. Joseph
    Josefina (Sp.); Josephine, Fifi, Fifine (Fr.)
Josette (Fr.) pet Josephine
Josiane (Fr.) combination Joseph and Anne
Josie (Fr.) fem. Joseph
Joslyn (L) just, honest
    Justine, Josseline, Joscelin, Josceline (Fr.); Justina, Jocelyn
Josse (Fr.) var. Jessie, Joyce
Joy (OFr.) jewel, delight
    Joia
Joya (Sp.) jewel
Juana (Sp.) fem. John
    Juanita, Jone; Yoana (Basque)
Judi (Navajo Indian) antelope
Judith (Heb.) praised
    Juditha, Judit, Judy, Jody
Juillet (Fr.) July
Julia (L) youth; fem. Julius
    Julie, Julienne, Juliette, Julitte, Julienne (Fr.); Juliana, Julie, Juliet, Giula, Giulia, Biulietta (It.); Julia, Juliana, Julita, Julieta (Sp.); Juliane, Jill, Jillian, Gill, Gillian, Sheila (Irish); Yulene, Julene (Basque)
Jumanah (Arab.) pearl
Jun (Japanese) obedient
June (L) youthful; fem. Junius
    Juin (Fr.)
Juno (L) Roman goddess, guardian of women
Jurisa (Slav.) storm
Justine (L) just; fem. Justin
    Justina
Jutta (L) near
Jyoti (Hindi) light
    Jyotsua

K

Kaatje (Dut.) Katherine
Kabira (Arab.) powerful
Kaedé (Japanese) maple leaf
Kaethe (Ger.) Katherine
Kagami (Japanese) mirror
Kai (Navajo Indian) willow tree
Kaïe (Celt., Fr.) combat
Kairos (Gk.) goddess born last to Jupiter
Kaiyo (Japanese) forgiveness
Kalamit (Heb.) flower
Kaley—var. Kelly
Kalonice (Gk.) beauty's victory
Kalyca (Gk.) rosebud
Kama (Japanese) sickle
Kamé (Japanese) tortoise (wish for longevity)
Kaméyo (Japanese) generations of the tortoise
Kamra (Arab.) moon
Kana (Japanese) written character of the alphabet
Kané (Japanese) bronze
Kanokporn (Thai) pure gold
Kanya (Thai) young lady
Kaoru (Japanese) fragrant
Kara (Gk.) short Katherine
Karelle (Fr.) var. Carin
Karen—short Katherine
    Karin, Karina, Karena, Carin, Carine, Caren,
    Carina
Karima (Arab.) generous
Karla—fem. Karl
Karleen—pet Karla
    Karlene
Karmele (Basque) Carmen

Karmia (Heb.) vineyard of the Lord
  Karmit, Karmelit, Karmel, Carmel, Carmella
Kasen (Dan.) Katherine
Kata (Japanese) worthy
Katherine (Gk.) pure
  Katharine, Kathryn, Kathie, Kate, Kathleen
  (Irish); Katrina (Scand.); Catalina (Sp.); Katarin,
  Kattalin (Basque); Katrine, Katrin, Kit, Kittie,
  Kitty, Katina, Kati, Katya, Katri, Kay, Kasia
  (Pol.); Ketty, Kelly Kay, Karen, Kara, Kaatje
  (Dut.); Kasen (Dan.)
Katsu (Japanese) victorious
Kay (Gk.) rejoice; (Teut.) fortified place; (L) gay;
  short Katherine
  Kaye
Kayla (Heb.) crown; (Yiddish) Celia
  Kaile, Kayl, Kaylee, Kayley, Kelila, Kelula
  (Heb.); Kele (Yiddish)
Kazashi (Japanese) hair ornament
Kazu (Japanese) great number, wish for longevity
Kefira (Heb.) young lion
Kei (Japanese) respectful, rapture, delight
Kelda (ONorse) fountain
Kelly (Irish, Teut.) farm by the spring; var. Catherine
Kendra (A-S) knowing
Kenna (OE) head, children; (ONorsc) knowledge
  Kendra, Kendis
Kennocha (Celt., Fr.) beauty
Keren (Heb.) horn
  Keryn
Keret (Heb.) city
Kerrie (OE) name of king, used also as girl's name
  Kerry
Ketty (Fr.) var. Catherine
Keturah (Heb.) fragrance
Khalida (Arab.) immortal, everlasting
Khalipha (Arab.) successor
Khaliqa (Arab.) nature
Khatiyba (Arab.) orator

Khayriyah (Arab.) good
Khin (Burmese) lovable
Kifle (Ethiopian) my class
Kikuë (Japanese) chrysanthemum branch
Kikumo (Japanese) chrysanthemum field
Kimi (Japanese) sovereign, peerless
Kimimela (Sioux Indian) butterfly
Kin (Japanese) gold
Kina (Gk., Swiss) Christian
Kinu (Japanese) silk cloth
Kiran (Hindi) ray
Kirstie (Scot.) nickname for Christine
Kishi (Japanese) beach, shore
Kiyo (Japanese) happy generations, pure
Kiyoshi (Japanese) clear, bright, beautiful
Ko (Japanese) chime, filial piety, fine
Kohana (Japanese) little flower
Koko (Blackfoot Indian) night
Kolete (Basque) Colette
Kolina (Gk., Swed.) pure
Komé (Japanese) rice
Kora (Fr., Gk.) young girl; in Greek myth, daughter of
    Jupiter and Demeter
    Koré
Kordel (Celt.) jewel of the sea
    Kordule, Cordelia
Koren (Gk.) maiden
Koto (Japanese) harp
Kozakura (Japanese) little cherry tree
Krista (Swiss) Christine
    Kristal, Kristel
Kristell (Fr.) var. Christine
Kuma (Japanese) bear
Kumi (Japanese) braid
Kuni (Japanese) capital city, province
Kura (Japanese) treasure house
Kurano (Japanese) storehouse field
Kuri (Japanese) chestnut
Kurva (Japanese) mulberry tree

L

Laberiane (Fr., OGer.) fem. Lambert
Labiba (Arab.) wise
Lacinia (Fr. from L) var. Lucie
Lada (Russ.) mythological goddess of beauty
Laélia (Fr. from L) sweeten
Lakshmi—Hindu goddess of fortune
Lalage (Gk.) talkative
Laleh (Persian) tulip
Lalita (Sanskrit) candid; (Gk.) talkative
Lamia (Fr. from OGer.) fem. Lambert
Lamya (Arab.) dark lips
Lana (Fr., Gk., Slav.) var. Helen
Landa (Basque) name for Virgin Mary
Lara (Russ. from L) famous; (Gk.) seagull
Larentia (L) foster mother of Romulus and Remus
Larina (L) seagull
Laris (L) cheerful
    Larice, Larissa
Larissa (Russ. from L) cheerful; (Gk.) seagull
Latona (L) Roman goddess
Laura (L) laurel
    Laure, Laurence, Laurentine, Laurelle, Laurette,
    Laurel, Lorel, Lorelle (Fr.); Laurie (Scot.); Lau-
    retta, Laurenza, Lorenya, Lara (It.); Lori (Swiss);
    Lovre (Slav.); Laurenzia, Laurana, Larunda, Lau-
    rencia (Sp.)
Laurel (L) laurel
    Lorel, Lorelle, Laureen
Laurice (L) laurel
    Loris
Laurie—var. Laura

Lavena (Celt., Fr.) joy
Laverne (OFr.) spring
    Laverna
Lavina—Roman mythological figure, mother of Rome;
    in Greek, wife of Aeneas
    Lavinia
Lawan (Thai.) pretty
Layla (Arab.) night
    Laila
Lea (Heb.) weary; fem. Leo
    Leah
Leccia (Fr.) var. Lucie
Lechsinska (Pol.) woodland spirit; fem. Lech
Leda (Gk.) in Greek mythology, mother of Castor and
    Pollux
Legarra (Basque) name for Virgin Mary
Leigh (OE) meadow
    Lee
Leila (Heb.) night
    Lelia, Lela, Lelah, Layla, Laila
Leli (Swiss) var. Magdalene
Lelia (Gk.) fair speech
    Lelie, Lelika
Léliane (Fr.) var. Leah
    Léa
Lemma (Ethiopian) developed
Lemuela (Heb.) fem. Lemuel
Lena (Gk.) light
    Lenka (Slav.); Lina, Lenia
Lenita (L) gentle
    Leneta
Lenmana (Hopi Indian) flute girl
Leocadia (Sp. from Gk.) lionlike
    Léocadie (Fr.)
Leola (It.) var. Cecilia; (L) lionlike
Leona (It., Sp.) lion
    Léone, Léonella, Léonie, Léonilde, Léonine (Fr.)
Leonora (Gk.) light

Leonore, Lenora, Lenore, Lenor, Leonila, Nilla, Linell

Leontine (L) lionlike
Leontyne

Leor (Heb.) I have light
Leore, Leora

Leora (Gk.) light

Lerzan (Turk.) trembling, shivering

Leshem (Heb.) precious stone

Leslie (Celt.) gray fort; var. Elizabeth

Letitia (L) gladness
Letizia (It.), Lettice (Fr.); Letticia, Letty, Lettie, Leta, Letta

Lévana (Celt., Fr.) joy

Lexine (Gk.) var. Alexine
Lexane

Leyla (Turk.) night

Lia (Heb., It.) dependence; (Heb.) var. Leah; short Julia
Lea

Liada (Slav.) mythological goddess of soldiers

Liana (Sp.) var. Juliana; (L) bond
Leana, Liane

Libby (Heb.) var. Elizabeth
Libbie

Liberata (L) freed

Licha (Sp.) var. Alicia

Lida (Slav.) people's love

Ligia (Gk.) silver voice

Lila (Persian, Sp.) bluish, azure

Lilia (Gk., L) pure; (Sp.) pure as a lily

Lilian (L) lily
Liliane (Fr.); Lillian, Lila, Lilah, Lilia, Lilly, Lillie, Lil, Lill, Lillis, Lilice

Lilith—legendary wife of Adam before Eve; ancient legendary evil spirit; var. Elizabeth

Lina (It., Sp. from Gk.) light

Linda (Sp.) beautiful

Lindsay (Teut.) island of serpents

Linette (Celt.) graceful; dim. Lina and Lea
    Lynette
Linnet (L) songbird
Liron (Heb.) song is mine
Lisa (Heb.) dim. Elizabeth
    Lise, Lisette (Fr.); Lizette, Liza, Lizzie, Lisil,
    Lisilka (Russ.); Lisi, Lisbetta, Liseta
Lisandra—fem. var. Alexander
Lisbeth—var. Elizabeth
Lise—var. Elizabeth
    Lisette (Fr. dim.)
Liubov (Russ.) love
    Liuba, Lioba, Luba, Liubima, Liubka (Russ.)
Liuva (Sp.) Liuba
Livia (L) first Roman empress; short Olivia
    Livie
Liyna (Arab.) tender
Lizzie—var. Elizabeth
Loélia (Fr.) var. Clélia
Lois—short Louisa
Lola (Sp.) dim. Carlota, Dolores
    Lolita, Loieta, Lotte (Ger.); Lotta (Swed.); Lotty,
    Lottie
Loma (Fr.) var. Salomé
    Lomée, Loménie
Lona (OE) single
Lora—var. Eleonore, Laura
Lore (Basque) Flora
Lorelei (OGer.) siren
Lorelle (Fr. from L) dim. Laura
    Lorella, Lorilla
Lorena (Sp.) laurel; (Fr.) from Lorraine, in France
Lorin—var. Laura
    Loren, Lauren
Lorinda—var. Laura
    Laurinda
Lorna—var. Lorena, Laura
Lorraine (OGer.) famous in battle; (Fr.) region in
    France

171

Lotty—dim. Charlotte
    Lotte, Lotta, Lottie
Lotus—Egyptian, lily of the Nile
Louella—var. Louise
Louisa—fem. Louis
    Louise, Heloise, Eloise, Louisiane (Fr.); Luella,
    Louella, Lulu, Lulita, Lois, Lisette, Loys, Luisa
    (It., Sp.); Lovisa (Slav.)
Lourdes (Fr., Sp.) shrine of the Virgin Mary
    Lorda (Basque)
Louve (Fr.) wolf
    Lua
Lubmila (Russ.) loving
Lubna (Arab.) flexible
Lucelia (Sp.) combination Luz and Celia
Lucia (It. from L) light
Lucille (Fr. from L) light
Lucrèce (Fr. from L) brings light
    Lucrecia (Sp.); Lucretia
Lucy (L) light
    Luca, Lucia, Luciana (It.); Luz (Sp.); Lucza
    (Hung.); Lucie, Lucienne, Lucille, Luce (Fr.);
    Lucceia, Lucette, Luciola, Luciole, Lucie, Lucin-
    da, Lucilla, Lucina
Ludmila (Russ.) people's love, loved by the people
    Mila, Luda, Milena, Milina, Lida
Lulu (Arab.) pearl
Lurline—var. Lorelei
Luzviminda—name created in the Philippines by com-
    bining parts of the names of the main islands
Lycoris (Gk.) twilight
Lydia (Gk.) ancient province in Asia Minor; (Arab.)
    strife
    Lydie (Fr.)
Lynn (A-S) cascade; var. Adeline
    Linn
Lyra (Gk.) harp, harmony
Lyris—var. Elizabeth
Lysa—var. Elizabeth

M

Mabel (L) lovable
 Mabelle
Macaria (Sp.) fem. Macario
Macawi (Sioux Indian) generous, motherly
Macella—var. Marcella
Macha (Fr.) var. Marie; (Sioux Indian) aurora
Machi (Japanese) ten thousand thousand (wish for longevity)
Madaan (Arab.) striving
Madalen (Basque) Madeline
Madde (Pol.) Magdala
Maddy—var. Madeleine
Madel (Heb.) tower; short Magdalen, Madeleine
Madeleine (Heb.) tower
 Madeline, Madeleine, Madelonnette, Mado (Fr.);
 Madelene, Madelena, Maidel, Madelyn, Madelon, Magdala; Maga, Maeli (Swiss); Madalen, Maialen, Malen (Basque)
Madge (Gk.) pearl; short Margaret
Madhur (Hindi) sweet
Madison (Teut.) Maud's son
Madiyha (Arab.) praiseworthy
Madra (It.) mother
Madruyna (Fr. from L) married woman
Mae (Heb.) bitter; var. Margaret, May
 May, Maya, Maia
Maëlle (Celt., Fr.) princess
Maena (Fr.) var. Marie
Maera (Fr.) var. Marie
Magali—var. Margarita
 Magaly
Magan (Teut.) power

Magda (Ger.) Magdalena
Magdala (Heb.) Magdalena, Magdalen
Magdi (Arab.) my glory
Magen (Heb.) protector
Maggie (Scot. from Gk.) dim. Margaret
    Maggy
Magia—var. Margaret
    Magiane
Magna (L) great
Magnolia (Fr.) tree named for Magnol, French botanist
Mahala (Heb.) tenderness
    Mahalia
Maharisha (Fr., Hindi) var. Marie
Mahesh (Hindi) god
Mai (Swed. from Gk.) pearl; (Navajo Indian) coyote
Maïa (Fr.) var. Marie
Maida (A-S) maiden
    Mayda
Maira (Welsh) Mary; (Sp. from L) marvelous
    Maire (Welsh)
Maisie (Scot.) Margaret
Maite (Basque) name for Virgin Mary, Maria del Amor
Maïte (Fr.) short Marie-Thérèse
    Maïténa
Maitland (OE) meadowland
Majida (Arab.) glorious, praiseworthy
Maka (Sioux Indian) earth
Makda (Ethiopian) Magda
Makemba—Congolese goddess
Mala (OE) meeting place
Malaine (Fr.) var. Madeleine
Malen (Basque) Magdalen
Mali (Thai) flower
Malika (Arab.) queen; also var. Marie
Malina (Heb.) tower
    Malin (Dut.)
Malka (Heb.) queen
Mallia (Fr.) var. Amelia
Malva (Gk.) soft

Malvina (Celt.) handmaiden
  Malvy, Malvane, Malva, Melva, Melvina
Manda (Slav.) Magdala; (L) lovable; short Amanda
  Mandelina
Mandy—short Amanda
Mangnoi (Thai) slender
Manon (Fr.) Magdalena, Marion, Mary
  Manette
Manuela (It., Sp.) fem. Manuel
Mapia (Sioux Indian) sky, heavenly
Mara (Heb.) bitter; var. Mary, Mareria
  Marah, Maralee, Marylyn, Marline, Marla, Marilla, Marella, Marieta
Maraam (Arab.) aspiration
Maralla—var. Mareria
Maramba—Congolese goddess of truth
Maravilla (Sp.) admirable
Marcella—fem. Marcel, Mark
  Marciane, Marcelle, Marcelline, Marcie, Marcilen, Marcelyn, Martine (Fr.); Marcia, Marcella (It.); Martia (Swiss); Martina (It., Slav.)
Mardeth—var. Martha
Mardi—pet Martha
Marea (L) of the sea; var. Mary
Maren (L) sea
  Marena, Marina, Maryn, Marnie, Marnya
Marenda—var. Miranda
Mareria (L) of the sea
Marga (Sp.) short Margarita
Margalide (Fr.) var. Margaret
Margalo—var. Margaret
  Margolo, Margery, Marjorie, Margot, Madge
Marganne (Fr.) var. Margaret
Margaret (Gk.) pearl
  Margarita, Marguerite, Margot, Margaux (Fr.); Margo, Meta, Meg, Mag, Madge, Margit, Greta (Scand.); Gredel, Gretchen (Ger.); Marga, Margalide, Marjory, Margery, Margolo, Margery, Peg, Peggy, Daisy

Mariam (Heb.) bitter; (Persian) flower name
  Marion (Scot.); Marianna, Masha (Russ.); Mariana (Port., Sp.); Mariedel (Slav.); Marieke (Dut.); Mariel, Marike (Ger.); Marietta (It.); Marynia, Marysia (Pol.)
Marianne (Heb.) rebellious; var. Mary
  Marian, Marion, Marianna
Mariannick (Fr.) combination Marie and Annick
Maribel (L) beautiful Mary
  Maribelle
Marice—var. Mary
  Marise, Marisse, Mariel, Marielle, Moira, Moyra
Maricruz (Sp.) combination Mary and cruz (cross)
  Mariluz—Maria de la Luz (light)
  Marisa—Maria Luisa
  Marisol—Maria de Sol (sun)
  Maritere—Maria Teresa
Mariel—var. Mary
  Marielle
Marietta (It.) pet Mary
  Mariette (Fr.)
Marigold—flower name (originally Mary's gold)
Marika—var. Mary
Marilda (Ger., Sp.) famous
Marilyn—var. Mary
Marina (L) sea maid
  Marnia, Marena, Maren, Marine, Marinette, Marisca
Mariyan (Arab.) purity
Marjan (Persian) coral
Marjaneh (Arab.) coral
Marjolaine (Fr.) flower name
Marjorie—var. Margaret
  Margery, Marsie
Marlena (Heb.) Magdala
  Marlène (Fr., Ger.)
Marmariyn (Arab.) alabaster
Marnin (Heb.) one who creates joy, one who sings

Maroussia—var. Margarita
Marpessa—var. Marie
Marret (Gk.) pearl
    Maretta, Marsali (Gaelic); Marusha (Slav.)
Marta (It.) bitter
Martha (Heb.) bitter; (Aramaic) lady
    Marta (It., Sp.); Marthe (Fr.)
Martine—fem. Martin
    Martina, Martella
Maru (Japanese) round
Mary (L) star of the sea; (Heb.) bitter
    Marie, Marielle, Mariette, Marice, Marise,
    Marilyse, Maryvonne, Manon (Fr.); Maria, Mara,
    Mariana, Marietta, Marea (It., Sp.); Marisha,
    Marishka, (Slav.); Maryk, Marek (Dut.); Mae,
    May (Scot.); Masha (Russ.); Marya, Mariar,
    Mariel, Marella, Marilla, Maraline, Marily, Moya,
    Maire, Minnie, Marylise, Maryse, Marica,
    Marisca, Marja, Marija
Marya (Arab.) purity, bright whiteness
Maryam (Arab.) purity
Masa (Japanese) straightforward, upright
Masago (Japanese) sand
Masha (Russ.) Mary
    Masheva
Massa (Arab.) uplifting
Massima (It., L) greatest
Masu (Japanese) increase
Masue (Japanese) branch of increase
Mathena (Fr.) combination Marie and Thérèse
Matilda (Teut.) mighty in battle
    Tilda, Tilly, Tillie, Matty, Mattie, Maud, Maude
Matsu (Japanese) pine, strong old age
Matsue (Japanese) pine branch
Matsuko (Japanese) pine tree
Mattiyaasa (Arab.) gift of God; fem. Matthew
Maude (Teut.) heroine; var. Madeleine, Matilda
Mauna (L) great

Maura (It., Sp.) dark; fem. Mauro, Maurice
    Maure, Maurette, Mauricette (Fr.); Mavra
    (Russ.)
Maureen (L) dark; (Celt.) great
    Maurine, Moreen
Maurelle (L) dark and elfin
Mauricia—fem. Maurice
    Meurisse, Maura, Mavra
Maurita (L) dark
Mave (Irish) mirth
Mavelle (Fr.) lovable; (Celt.) songbird, joy
    Mavie, Mave
Maxine (L) greatest
    Maximilienne, Maximiliane, Maxime (Fr.)
May (Scot.) short Margaret; (Heb.) bitter; also name
    of month
    Mai, Maya, Maja, Maisy, Maia
Maya (Hindi) mythological figure; (Gk.) mother,
    grandmother
Maybelle (Fr.) May; var. Mabel
Mayoree (Thai) beautiful
Meara (Irish) merry
Médé (Fr.) my delight
Medea (Gk.) ruler, pensive
Medora—poetic character of Lord Byron
Megan (A-S) strong
Megara (Gk.) first wife of Hercules
Meharene (Ethiopian) forgive us
Mehetabel (Heb.) beneficent, favored by God
    Mettabel
Mehri (Persian) kind, sunny, lovable
Meit (Burmese) affection
Melanell (Celt.) money
Melania (Gk., It.) black
Melanie (Fr., Gk.) black; (Celt.) princess
    Melany, Melony, Melonie, Mélia, Melina, Me-
    linda, Melania, Malania
Melantha (Gk.) dark flower

Melba—short Esmeralda, Emelda
Melicent (Teut.) industrious
    Melisenda (Sp.)
Melinda (Sp. from Gk.) love song; var. Amelinda,
    combination Amelia and Linda
Melior (L) better
Melisenda (Sp. from OGer.) strong
Melissa (Gk.) honeybee
    Melisse, Melita, Meletta, Melitta, Lissa
Mellaky (Arab.) princess
Melle (Celt., Fr.) princess
Mellesse (Ethiopian) returned
Melodie (Fr.) melody; var. Odile
    Melody, Melodine
Melva (Celt.) chief
Mendi (Basque) name for Virgin Mary
Menelea (Sp.) fem. Menelaus (Gk.) husband of Helen
    of Troy
Mérane (Fr.) dim. Emmerane
    Mérana
Meraud (Gk.) emerald
Merav (Heb.) daughter of Saul in Bible
Mercedes (Sp. from L) favors, rewarding, liberator,
    reference to Virgin Mary
    Mercede (It.); Mecha (Sp. dim.)
Mercia (A-S) ancient kingdom
Mercy (L) merciful
Meredith (Celt.) sea protector
Meriel (Gk.) myrrh; var. Muriel
    Merriel
Meris (L) of the sea
    Maris, Marisse, Merisse, Merice
Merle (L) blackbird
Merlyn (Celt., Sp.) sea hill
    Merlina
Merovée (Fr. from Ger.) holy fame
Merrell (Teut.) famous
    Merrill, Meryl, Merryl, Meryll, Merile

Merriel—var. Muriel
Meryl (Arab.) myrrh
   Meriel
Messaline (Fr.) from Messina, in Italy
   Messalina
Meta (Ger., Gk.) pearl; dim. Margaret, Almeta
   Mette (Dan.)
Metea (Gk.) gentle
Meurisse (Fr., L) Moorish
Mevena (Celt., Fr.) agile
Mica (Heb.) like the Lord
   Micah, Meecah
Micheline (Fr.) var. Michelle
Michelle (Heb.) who is like God
   Michele, Micheline, Michée, Michon, Michaela
   (Fr.); Mikele (Basque); Micaela, Miguela, Migu-
   elita (Sp.); Michaela (It.); Michaila, Michajla,
   Miha (Slav.)
Michi (Japanese) the way
Michiko (Japanese) three thousand
Midori (Japanese) green
Mië (Japanese) triple branch
Mieral (Ger., Heb.) bitter
   Molly, Mija
Migina (Omaha Indian) returning moon
Migisi (Chippewa Indian) eagle
Mignon (Fr.) darling
Mika (Japanese) new moon
Mikazuki (Japanese) moon of the third night
Miki (Japanese) stem
Mikie (Japanese) main branch
Mila (Slav.) lovely; (L) work; (Sp.) short Milagros
Milagros (Sp.) miracles, name for Virgin Mary, Our
   Lady of Miracles
   Mila, Milagritos
Milagrosa (Sp.) miraculous
Milcah (Heb.) queen
   Malka

Mildred (A-S) mild, gentle counselor; gentle speech
Milly, Millie

Milena (Heb.) var. Ludmila, Magdalena; combination
Marie and Helen
Milène (Fr.)

Milia (Basque) Emily

Milicent (Teut.) strength
Melecent, Melicent, Milly, Millie

Mimi (Fr. from Teut.) resolute, strong; dim. Wilhelmina, Miriam
Minella, Minette, Minne (Ger.); Minka (Pol.)

Mimiteh (Omaha Indian) new moon

Mina (Ger.) short Wilhelmina; (Persian) blue sky;
(Arab.) harbor; (Japanese) south
Minami (Japanese)

Minaku (Blackfoot Indian) berry woman

Minal (Delaware Indian) fruit

Minau (Persian) heaven

Miné (Japanese) peak

Minéko (Japanese) mountain range

Minerva—Roman goddess of wisdom and the arts

Mingala (Scot.) soft and fair

Mini (Sioux Indian) water

Minna (Teut.) loving memory; short Wilhelmina
Minnie

Minya (Osage Indian) elder sister

Mirabelle (L) wondrous beauty
Mira

Miranda (Sp. from L) deserving admiration, admirable
Marenda

Mireille (Fr.) miraculous; var. Marie, Miranda
Mireya (Sp.)

Miren (Basque) var. Maria

Miriam (Heb.) bitter, rebellious
Mimi, Miri, Mitzi

Mirna (Sp.) sad

Mirta (Gk., Sp.) crown of beauty
Mirtala, Myrta

Mirza (Persian) lady
Misae (Osage Indian) white sun
Misao (Japanese) honor, wifely fidelity
Mitena (Omaha Indian) coming moon
Mitra (Persian) name of angel
Mitsu (Japanese) light
　　Mitsuko
Mitsuë (Japanese) shining branch
Miya (Japanese) temple
Miyna (Arab.) harbor
Miyoko (Japanese) beautiful generations
Miyuki (Japanese) deep snow, tranquillity and beauty,
　　calm silence
Modestine (Fr.) modest
　　Modesty, Modesta (Sp.); Modeste, Modestie
Moina (Scot.) soft; (Celt.) gentle
　　Moyna
Moira (Celt.) great
Molly—dim. Mary
Molara (Basque) name for Virgin Mary
Mon (Japanese) gate
Mona (Irish) noblewoman; (L) single; var. Monique
Monacella (L) little nun
Moncha—dim. Ramona
Monica (It., Sp.) adviser, single; short Dominica
　　Monique (Fr.); Monika, Monike (Ger.); Moni
Mora—var. Maura
　　Morane, Morée (Fr.)
Morgan (Celt.) sea dweller
　　Morgane, Morgance (Fr.); Morgana
Moria—character in Ben Jonson's *Cynthia's Revels*
Morie (Japanese) bay
Morna (Celt.) gentle, beloved
Motaza (Arab.) proud
Moya (Celt.) great
Moyna—var. Monique
Mrena (Slav.) white eyes
Muguette (Fr.) flower name
Mükerrem (Turk.) honorable, venerable, honored

Muna (Arab.) wish
Munira (Arab.) luminous
Mura (Japanese) village
Murasaki (Japanese) purple
Muriel (Gk.) myrrh, perfume; (Heb.) bitter
    Murielle, Myra, Meriel (Fr.)
Murimi (Kikuyu, Kenya) farmer
Murugi (Kikuyu, Kenya) cook
Myra (Gk.) myrtle; (L) wonderful
    Myrta, Myrena, Mira, Myrilla, Mirilla, Mireille,
    Mireya
Myrtle (L) myrtle
    Myrtille
Mysie (Scot.) pearl

N

Naamah (Heb.) pleasant, beautiful
    Namana
Naamit (Heb.) bird
Naava (Heb.) beautiful
Nabeela (Arab.) noble
    Nabila
Nabrissa (Fr., Gk.) peace
Nada (Slav.) hope
    Nadezna, Nadezhda, Naia, Nadya, Nadia, Na-
    dine, Nadège (Slav.)
Nadda (Arab.) generosity
Nadette (Fr.) dim. Bernadette
Nadine (Fr.) dim. Bernadine
    Nada
Nadira (Arab.) rare, precious
Naeva (Fr.) var. Eve
Nafisa (Arab.) precious
Nagida (Heb.) nobility

Nahed (Arab.) beautiful
Nahid (Persian) Venus; (Arab.) elevated
Nahimana (Sioux Indian) mystic
Naia (Gk.) flowing
 Naied, Naida, Naya
Naiara (Basque) name for Virgin Mary
Naila (Arab.) favor
Naïla (Fr. from L) winged
Naja (Arab.) success
Najam (Arab.) star
Najia (Arab.) wholesome
Najiba (Arab.) excellent, noble heroine
Najila (Arab.) wide eyes, brilliant eyes
Najma (Arab.) star
Nala (Arab.) drink
Namaama (Arab.) mint plant
Namah (Heb.) beautiful, pleasant
 Nama
Nami (Japanese) wave
 Namiko
Namid (Chippewa Indian) dancer
Nan (Heb.) grace; dim. Hannah, Ann
 Nana, Nancy, Nanette, Nanelle, Nanine, Nanetta,
 Nanelia, Nanny, Nanda, Nandina
Nana—var. Anne
Nandelle (Ger.) adventuring life
Naomi (Heb.) pleasant, sweet
 Naoma
Nara (Gk.) happy; (OE) north; (Japanese) oak
Narcisse (Fr., Gk.) daffodil
 Narcisa (Sp.); Narkissa (Russ.)
Narda (Gk.) plant name; var. Nara
Nardine—dim. Bernardine
Narmada (Hindi) gives pleasure
Nascha (Navajo Indian) owl
Nasia (Heb.) miracle of God
 Nasya
Nasiba (Arab.) love, poetry
Nasima (Arab.) gentle breeze

Nasira (Arab.) helper
  Nasra
Nasrin (Arab.) wild rose
Nastagia (It. from Gk.) resurrection
  Nastassia (Russ.)
Nasuh (Arab.) pure
Nata (Sanskrit) dancer
Natalie (Fr.) Christmas child
  Natalia (Russ.); Natasha (Russ. dim.); Natalie,
  Natica, Natalena, Natalène (Fr.); Tali, Talie,
  Tasha, Noela, Nouel, Noelle, Nattie, Netty
Natara (Arab.) sacrifice
Nathania (Heb.) fem. Nathan
  Natania
Natividad (Sp.) birth, nativity
Nazanin (Persian) delightful
Nazira (Arab.) overseer
Neala—fem. Neal
Neda (Slav.) Sunday's child
  Nedelka, Nedana
Nedda—fem. dim. Edward
Neelam (Hindi) sapphire
Nefertiti—Egyptian queen; the beautiful one has come
Ne Htun (Burmese) sunshine
Neige (Fr.) snow
Nelia—short Cornelia
Nell (Gk.) light; var. Noel, Eleanor; dim. Helen
  Nelly, Nellie, Nellis, Nellice, Nelma
Nella—var. Helen, Noël
Nelle (Gk.) stone
Nelly (Gk.) light; dim. Eleanor, Helen, Noël
Neoma (Gk.) new moon
Nereida (Gk.) sea nymph
Nerina (Sp.) sea nymph
  Nerine
Nerissa (Gk.) of the sea
  Nerita
Nese (Gk.) pure; var. Agnes
  Neza, Neys, Nessie

Nessa (ONorse) promontory; (Russ.) short Agnessa
Nesha, Nessia, Netia
Nesta (Welsh) pet Agnes
Neta (Heb.) plant
Netania (Heb.) gift of God
Netanya, Nethania, Natania, Nathania
Netta (Scot.) pet Janet
Nettie—pet Antoinette, Natalie
Netty
Neva (Sp.) snow; (OE) new
Nevada (Sp.) snowy
Neylan (Turk.) fulfilled wish
Neysa (Gk., Sp.) var. Agnes
Niabi (Osage Indian) fawn
Nicci (L) victory
Nichele (L) victory
Nichelle, Nicole, Nicolette, Nicoline, Nicola
Nicia (It.) fem. Nicholas; pet Berenice
Nicole (Fr.) fem. Nicholas
Nicolette (Fr. dim.); Nicoletta
Nida (Arab.) call
Nidawi (Omaha Indian) fairy girl
Nika (Slav.) Nicole
Nike (Gk.) victory, winged goddess in Greek mythology
Nilda (Ger.) short Brunhilda
Nildag (Turk.) blue mountain
Nilüfer (Turk.) lotus, water lily
Nima (Arab.) blessings; (Heb.) thread
Nina (Heb.) grace; var. Ann; (Sp.) little girl; (Russ.) pet Ninotchka, Ann
Nena, Ninette
Ninon (Sp. from Heb.) grace
Nanon
Ninovan (Cheyenne Indian) our home
Niobe (Gk.) fern
Nirel (Heb.) light of God
Niria (Heb.) plow
Nirit (Heb.) plant name

Nirmal (Hindi) pure
Nisa (Arab.) woman
Nissa (Heb.) sign, emblem; (Scand.) elf
Nita (Sp.) short Juanita, Anita
Nixie (OGer.) water sprite
Nizana (Heb.) flower bud
Noam (Arab.) happiness
Noelle (Fr.) Christmas
    Noella, Noël, Novela, Novelenn
Noëmie (Fr.) grace
Nofia (Heb.) panorama
    Nophia
Noga (Heb.) shining; morning light
Noïra (Fr.) var. Eleanor
Nola (Celt.) noble, famous; (L) olive; fem. Nolan
Nolita (L) olive
Noll—nickname Olive
Nolwenn (Celt.) white lamb
Nona (L) ninth
    Nonia, Nonie, Noni, Nonn
Noor (Persian) light
Nora (Gk.) light; (L) honor; (Irish) pet Eleanor,
    Leonora
    Noreen, Norah, Noria, Nore, Noriane, Noura
Noralma (Sp.) combination Nora and Alma
Norberta—fem. Norbert
Noriko (Japanese) precept
Norine (L) honor
    Norina, Noreen
Norma—fem. Norman
Norna (Norse) mythological goddess
Nova (L) new
    Novia
Noya (Heb.) ornament
Nu (Burmese) tender
Nui (Japanese) tapestry, embroidery
Nunciata (L) messenger; (Sp.) short Annunciata
    Nunzia (It.)
Nureen (Heb.) light

Nurit (Heb.) plant name
Nurita
Nuwa (Chinese) mythological character, mother goddess, creator of mankind and of order
Nuwnah (Arab.) dimpled chin
Nydia (L) refuge; (Sp.) nest
Nidia
Nyla—ancient Egyptian princess
Nympha (Sp.) sea nymph
Nyoko (Japanese) gem treasure
Nysa (Gk.) goal
Nyssa

O

Obelia (Gk.) needle
Octavia (L) eighth
Octave, Octavienne, Octavie (Fr.); Ocilia
Oda (Teut.) rich
Odeda (Heb.) strong
Odele (Gk.) melody
Odelete
Odelette (Fr.) little song
Odelia (Heb.) I will praise God; (Teut.) prosperous
Odila, Odile
Odera (Heb.) plough
Odette—pet Odele, Odile
Odetta
Odile (Fr., Ger.) rich
Odila (Ger.); Odeline, Odiane
Odina (Algonquin Indian) mountain
Ofelia (Sp.) Ophelia
Ofira (Heb.) gold
Ophira
Ofra (Heb.) young goat
Ola (ONorse) ancestor; fem. Olaf

Olga (Russ.) fem. Oleg
Olna, Olinka
Olimpia (Gk., It., Sp.) Olympian
Olympe (Fr.)
Olinda (Sp. from OGer.) protector of property; var.
Yolanda
Olive (L) olive, symbol of peace
Oliva
Olivia (Sp.) olive
Livia, Livy, Nola, Nollie, Olivette, Olivianne
Omaima (Arab.) small nation
Ona (OE) ash tree, river
Onaedo (Ibo tribe, Nigeria) gold
Ondina (Sp.) water spirit
Oona (Irish) one
Una, Juno
Opa (Choctaw Indian) owl
Opal (Sanskrit) precious stone
Opaline (Fr.)
Ophelia (Gk.) help, wisdom, serpent
Ofelia (Sp.); Ophélie (Fr.)
Ora (Heb.) light; (L) gold; short Honora, Eleanora
Orah, Orabelle, Orit
Oralee (Heb.) my light
Oralee, Orali, Orlee
Oralia (L) margin, golden
Orane (Fr.) rising
Oria (L) the East, golden
Oriana, Oriane
Oriel (OFr.) golden, name of bird
Orlantha (Teut.) fem. Orlando
Orlena (Fr.) gold
Orlene
Ormanda—fem. Armand
Orma
Orna (Heb.) light, cedar tree
Ornette (Heb.) light, cedar tree
Orpah (Heb.) fawn
Orquidea (Sp.) orchid

Orseline (Dut. from L) bear
Orsola (It. from L) bear; fem. Orson
    Ursula, Urseline
Ortensia (It. from L) guardian
    Hortense
Orva (OFr.) golden worth; (A-S) brave friend
Osanna (Heb.) thanks, praise to God
    Osanne (Fr.)
Osma—fem. Osmund
Ottalie (Swed.) fem. Otto
    Ottillie
Ottavia (It.) eighth
    Octavia
Otthild (Ger.) happy heroine
    Ottilia
Ottilia (OGer.) lucky heroine; fem. Otto
    Odila, Odile, Othilia, Othilie
Özçiçek (Turk.) flower essence

P

Paciane (Fr. from L) peace
Pacita (Sp.) dim. Paz
Pagana (Fr. from L) pagan, peasant
Page (Fr.) attendant on noble
Pallas (L) Roman goddess of wisdom; (Gk.) name for
    Athena
Palma (L) victory
    Palmyre
Palmira (Sp.) city of palms
Paloma (Sp.) dove
Pamela—name made fashionable in romantic novels;
    (Gk.) friend, all and honey
Pandora (Gk.) gifted
Pansy (OFr.) thought, flower name

Panthea (Gk.) of all the gods
Paola (It.) little
Paquita (Sp.) dim. Frances
Parasha (Russ.) girl born on Good Friday
Pari (Persian) fairy, eagle
Parnell—var. Petronella
Parthenia (Gk.) maidenly
Parvaneh (Persian) butterfly
Pascale (Heb.) passover; (Fr.) Easter
    Pascaline (Fr.); Pasha (Russ.)
Pastora (Sp.) fem. Pastor
Patience (L) patience
    Paciencia (Sp.)
Patricia (L) noble, wellborn
    Patrizia (It.); Patriciane (Fr.); Patria, Patsy, Pattie,
    Patty, Tricia, Trisha
Paula (L) little; (Gk.) rest
    Paola (It.); Paule, Pauline, Paulette (Fr.); Paulita,
    Polla, Polly
Paz (Sp.) peace
Pazi (Ponca Indian) yellow bird
Pearl (L) pear, gem name
    Perle, Perlette (Fr.)
Peggy—dim. Margaret
Pellkita (Basque) Felicity
Penela (Fr.) var. Helen
Penelope (Gk.) weaver, wife of Ulysses, symbol of
    fidelity
    Penny
Penta (L) blessed
Penthea (Gk.) fifth
Peony (Gk.) flower name
Pepita (Sp.) fem. dim. Joseph
Perdita (L) lost
Pernelle (Fr.) fem. dim. Peter
Persephone (Gk.) flower name, Greek mythological
    symbol of renewal and fertility after hard times
Peta (Blackfoot Indian) golden eagle
Petra—fem. Peter

Perrine, Pierrette, Petronille, Petronelle (Fr.);
Petrina (Scot.); Petronella (Ger.); Petrushka, Pet-
rinka (Russ.); Kepe (Basque); Perette, Pernette,
Pet

Petrina (Gk.) fem. Peter

Petronella (L) stone; fem. var. Peter

Phaedra—Greek mythological figure, wife of Theseus

Phailin (Thai) sapphire

Pheodora (Russ.) fem. Theodore

Philana (Gk.) lover of mankind

Philippa (Gk.) lover of horses
Philippine (Fr.); Pippa (It.)

Phillida (Gk.) loving

Phillis (Gk.) foliage
Phyllis

Philomela (Gk.) nightingale
Philomel

Philomena—var. Philomela; fem. Philander
Filomena (It., Sp.); Philomène (Fr.)

Philumena (L) daughter of light

Phoebe (Gk.) shining, brilliant
Phoebé (Fr.); Phebe, Febe

Phyllis (Gk.) green leaf

Pia (It., Sp. from L) pious; (Hindi) loved one; fem.
var. Peter

Piedad (Sp.) Virgin Mary; (L) pity

Pilar (Sp.) name for Virgin Mary

Pimchan (Thai) like the moon

Pippa (It.) dim. Philippa

Pirimona (Gk.) loving thought

Placida (Sp.) serene
Placidia, Placidie (Fr.)

Pleasance (OE) pleasance

Polly—nickname Mary
Pollyanna

Poloma (Choctaw Indian) bow

Polyanthe (Gk.) blooming as many flowers

Pomona (Sp.) fruitful

Poppy—flower name
Portia—heroine of Merchant of Venice
Prabha (Hindi) light
Preeti (Hindi) love
Presentación (Sp.) reference to Virgin Mary
Prima (L) first
  Primalia
Primavera (Sp.) spring
Primrose (L) first rose
Prisana (Thai) question
Priscilla (L) the ancient
  Priscialiana (Sp.)
Prithvi (Hindi) earth
Prodigios (Sp.) reference to Virgin Mary
Prudence (L) prudent
  Prudencia (Sp.); Prudentia, Prudy, Pru, Prue
Prunella (OFr.) plum-colored; flower name
  Prunelle (Fr.)
Pureza (Sp.) purity
  Garbi (Basque)
Purificación (Sp.) purification
  Pura, Purisima, Garbiñe (Basque)
Purisima (Sp.) purest
  Pura

Q

Qadira (Arab.) powerful
  Kadira
Qamra (Arab.) moon
  Kamra
Qiturah (Arab.) fragrance
Queen (Teut.) woman, queen
  Queenie

Quenby (Scand.) womanly
Quinby (Scand.) from queen's estate
Quintana (L) fifth
Quiterie (Fr. from L) tranquil

R

Rabia (Arab.) fourth
Rachel (Heb.) lamb, gentle innocence
 Raquel (Fr., Sp.); Rachele (It.); Rahel (Pol.);
 Rahil (Russ.); Rachilde, Racilia, Ray, Rae
Rachida (Arab.) wise
 Rasheeda
Radcliff (OE) red cliff
Radiya (Arab.) content
Rafiqa (Arab.) sweetheart, companion
Rafiya (Arab.) high, uplifting
Rahab (Heb.) white cloud
Rahat (Arab.) rest, repose
Rahil (Arab.) traveler
Rahila (Arab.) exodus
Rahima (Arab.) merciful
Rai (Japanese) trust
Raïa (Fr., Gk.) peace
 Raïane
Raida (Arab.) leader
Raihannah (Arab.) sustenance
Raina (Teut.) mighty; (Fr.) queen
Raisa (Arab.) leader
Raïssa (Fr., Gk.) peace
Raja (Arab.) hope
Rajni (Hindi) night
Raku (Japanese) pleasure
Ramona—fem. Ramon
 Raimonda, Raymonde

Rana (Arab.) gaze; (Sanskrit) royal; (Fr.) var. Renée
    Rania
Randi (Scand., Teut.) wise, fair one
    Randy
Raniya (Arab.) gazing
Raphaela—fem. Raphael
    Rafaela
Rasha (Arab.) young gazelle
Rasia (Pol.) queen
Rasine (Pol.) rose
    Rashe, Rosa
Ratanaporn (Thai) crystal blessing
Rauline (Fr.) fem. Raul
Rauwth (Arab.) Ruth
Raymonda—fem. Raymond
    Raymonde, Raimonde
Rebecca (Heb.) binding, servant of God
    Rebeca, Reba, Becky
Regan (Celt., OFr.) royal
Regina (It., Sp.) queen
    Régine (Fr.); Raina, Rina, Gina, Reine, Reina
Rehana (Arab.) laurel
Rei (Japanese) propriety
Reine (Fr.) queen
    Régilla, Réjane
Reinelda (Ger.) fem. Reinaldo
    Renilde, Renilda
Rekha (Hindi) fine
Remedios (Sp.) remedy, reference to Virgin Mary
Ren (Japanese) arranger
Renana (Celt.) seal
Renata (It.) reborn
    Renate (Ger.); Renée, Renelle (Fr.)
Renita (L) firm
Réséda (Fr.) fragrant plant
Reta (Gk.) pearl
    Rita, Riti, Ritti
Retta (Ethiopian) won
Rhapsody (Gk.) weaver of songs

Rhea—Greek mythological figure, daughter of Uranus, mother of the gods
    Rea
Rhene (Gk.) lamb
Rhoda (Gk.) rose
    Rhodé (Fr.); Rhodocella
Rhomé (Fr.) power
Rhonada—district in South Wales
Ricarda (It., Sp.) fem. Ricardo
Rifqat (Arab.) Rebecca
Riku (Japanese) land
Rim (Arab.) gazelle
Rima (Arab.) white antelope
Rimma (Fr.) from Reims, France
Rina (Heb.) joy; var. Reine
    Rena
Rita (Gk., Sp.) pearl; dim. Magarita
    Irta (Basque)
Roberta—fem. Robert
    Robin, Robyn, Robinette
Robin—bird name; short Roberta
    Robine (Fr.)
Robina (Scot.) robin
Rocío (Sp.) covered with dew, dewdrops
Roda (Gk.) rose garland
Roderica—fem. Roderick
Rogelia (Sp.) fem. Roger
Rohini (Hindi) woman
Roku (Japanese) emolument
Rolanda—fem. Roland
    Rolande (Fr.); Orlanda
Romaine (Fr.) Roman
    Romane, Romana (Sp.); Manka
Romilda (Teut.) great heroine
    Romelda
Romola (L) strength, power, fame
Ronalda—fem. Ronald
Ronana—var. Renana
Rory (Celt.) red

Rosalba—combination Rose and Alba
Rosalie—combination Rose and Lily
    Rosalia, Rosalea
Rosalind (Sp.) beautiful one; combination Rose and
    Linda
    Roslyn, Rosalinda, Roslinde, Rozaline
Rosamond (L) rose of the world
Rosanne—rose of grace; combination Rose and Anne
Rosaura—breath of rose
Rose (L) Rose
    Rose, Rosette, Roselle, Rosine (Fr.); Rosa,
    Rosina, Rosalba, Roseta, Rosana (It., Sp.); Roza,
    Rozina (Slav.); Rosaria, Rosita, Rosalinda,
    Rosaclara, Rosamaria (Sp.); Rosabel, Rosalie,
    Rosanne, Rosalinde, Rosamunde (Ger.); Rose-
    mary, Rosalbanne, Rosée
Rosemary—combination Rose and Mary
    Rosemarie
Rowena (Celt.) white mane; (OE) famous friend
Roxana (Persian) dawn
    Roxane
Ruby (L) red, jewel name
Rufina (It., Sp. from L) red hair
Runa (Ger.) secret, mysterious
Ruqaya (Arab.) ascend
Ruri (Japanese) emerald
Ruth (Heb.) beauty, friend, vision
Rutilia (L) fiery red
Ryo (Japanese) dragon, generations
Ryu (Japanese) lofty

S

Saarah (Arab.) princess
Saba (Arab.) eastern wind, morning
Sabi (Arab.) young girl
Sabine (Fr. from L) Sabine, ancient people of Central
    Italy
    Sabina, Savina, Saby, Sabienne, Sabinka, Binelle
Sabira (Arab.) patient
Sabiya (Arab.) morning
Sabrina (A-S) princess
Sacha (Fr.) dim. Alexander
    Sasha
Sachi (Japanese) bliss
Sada (Japanese) chaste
    Sadako
Sadie (Heb.) princess; dim. Sarah
Sadira (Arab.) name of a star
Sadiya (Arab.) very lucky, fortunate
Saffi (Dan., Gk.) wisdom
Safia (Arab.) pure
Safuwra (Arab.) little bird
Sahkyo (Navajo Indian) mink
Sahlah (Arab.) smooth
Sai (Japanese) talented
Saida (Arab.) happy
Sajida (Arab.) prostrate
Sakaë (Japanese) prosperity
Sakina (Arab.) inspired, peace of mind
Salali (Cherokee Indian) squirrel
Saliha (Arab.) good
Salima (Arab.) safe
    Salma

Salina (Fr. from L) solemn, dignified
Sally (Heb.) princess; dim. Sarah
Salome (Heb.) peaceful
Salvadora (Sp.) fem. Salvador
Salviana (L) saved
    Salviane (Fr.); Salvina, Salvine
Sama (Arab.) generosity
    Samiyha
Samala (Heb.) fem. Samuel
Samantha (Heb.) established by God
Samara (Heb.) caretaker
Samia (Arab.) noble
Samira (Arab.) entertaining companion, amusing
Samiya (Arab.) elevated
Sancha (Sp.) holy
    Sancia (It.); Sancie (Fr.); Sanchia
Sandra—var. Alexandra
Sandrine—var. Alexandrine
Sanne (Dut., Heb.) lily
Sanseviéra (Fr.) flower name
Sapphira (Heb.) beautiful
Sapphire (Gk.) sapphire
Sarah (Heb.) princess
    Sara, Sarita, Sally, Sadie
Sarai (Heb.) quarrelsome
Saraid (Celt.) excellent
Sarita (Hindi) stream, river; (Sp.) little princess
Saroj (Hindi) like a lotus, morning
Sato (Japanese) sugar, home
Sauda (Arab.) black
Savine (Fr.) var. Sabine
Sawa (Japanese) marsh
Sawsan (Arab.) Susan
Sayada (Arab.) lady
Sâyan (Turk.) worthy, deserving
Sebastienne (Fr.) venerable
    Sebastiana (It., Sp.); Sebastene (Basque); Sebastiane (Fr.); Sebastia

Sebila (Sp.) wise old woman
    Sevilla (Sp.); Sibbel, Sibel, Sibella, Sibila, Sibyl,
    Sibylla, Sibille, Sibyle, Cybele (Fr.)
Seble (Ethiopian) cultivation
Secunda (L) second
Sefa (Swiss) dim. Josefa
Sefora (Heb., Sp.) bird
Ségolène (Fr. from OGer.) sweet victory
Sei (Japanese) force, truth
Seki (Japanese) barrier
Sela (Heb.) rock
    Seleta
Selam (Ethiopian) peace
Selena (Gk.) moon
    Selene, Céline, Séléné (Fr.); Selina (Sp.)
Selenia (Gk.) beautiful as the moon
    Selina
Selima (Heb.) peaceful; (Arab.) fem. Solomon
Selinde (Ger.) conquering snake
Selma (Celt.) fair, just
Selvaggia (It.) wild
Sema (Turk.) sky, heavens
Semiramis (Assyrian) friend of the doves
Sen (Japanese) being that lives for thousands of years
    and has magical powers
Senalda (Sp.) sign
Seniz (Turk.) joyful
Sephora (Heb.) beautiful
Septima (L) seventh
Serafina (It., Sp.) seraph; (Heb.) burning, ardent
    Seraphita, Serapia, Seraphine (Fr.)
Serena (It., Sp.) serene
    Sérène (Fr.)
Sergiane (Fr.) fem. Serge
    Sergine
Serilda (Teut.) armored heroine
Setsu (Japanese) tender and true
    Setsuko

Sevinç (Turk.) delight
Shabnan (Persian) raindrop
Shafiqa (Arab.) kindness
Shahdi (Persian) happy
Shahida (Arab.) witness
Shahina (Arab.) falcon
Shaira (Arab.) thankful
    Shakira
Shakila (Arab.) pretty
Shama (Arab.) candle wax
Shamima (Arab.) fragrant
Shanata (Hindi) peaceful
Sharan (Hindi) protection
Sharifa (Arab.) noble
Sharon (Heb.) plain
Shashi (Hindi) moonbeam
Shawn (Irish from Heb.) God's gracious gift
Sheba—short Bathsheba
Sheelah (Irish) Cecilia
    Sheila, Shelagh, Sheelagh, Shiela, Sheilag
Shelley (A-S) ledge meadow
Shere (Fr.) var. Cecile
Shereen (Arab.) sweet
Sherifa (Arab.) noblewoman
Shideh (Persian) sun
Shigé (Japanese) exuberant
Shina (Japanese) possessions, virtue
Shira (Heb.) song
    Sheera, Shirah
Shirley (OE) white meadow
    Shirlee, Shirlie, Sherley, Shirleen, Shirlene, Sheryl, Sheri, Sherry
Shirushi (Japanese) evidence
Shizuno (Japanese) quiet field
Shokofeh (Persian) bloom
Sholeh (Persian) flame
Shula (Arab.) flame, brightness
Sibley (A-S) friendly; var. Sibyl

Sibyl (Gk.) wise; (L) prophetic
Sibylle, Sibylline, Sibile, Sébile, Cibilla, Sibilla, Sébline, Cybèle (Fr.)

Sidonia (It.) ancient Phoenician city
Sido, Sidonie, Sidaine, Sidoine (Fr.); Sitta, Sidelle, Sydney

Sidra (L) starlike

Sigfreda (Ger.) fem. Siegfried
Siegfrida

Sigismonda (Ger., It.) fem. Siegmund
Siegmunda, Sigismonde, Zygmunda

Sigolène (Fr.) var. Ségolène
Sigolaine

Sigrada (Ger.) victory
Sigrade (Fr.); Sigrid (Scand.); Sigritt, Sigrin, Siri

Silana (Fr.) var. Solenne

Silenia (L) silent

Silva (L) woodland
Silvana (It.); Silvie, Silvine, Sylvie, Silviane, Silvina, Silva, Silvane (Fr.); Vestra, Sylvette, Silana, Silane

Silvia (It.) woodland
Sylvia, Silvana, Silva

Sima (Arab.) sign

Simin (Persian) silver

Simone (Fr.) fem. Simon
Simona (It., Sp.); Simonette, Syma

Sinopa (Blackfoot Indian) kit fox

Sinovia (Russ.) Zenobia

Sirana (Gk.) fem. Siran
Sirane

Sirena (Gk.) siren
Sirène (Fr.)

Sirida—fem. Siran

Sisay (Ethiopian) prosper

Sisley—var. Cecily

Sitareh—var. Esther

So (Burmese) naughty

Socorro (Sp.) help, reference to Virgin Mary
Sofia (Gk., Hung., It.) wisdom
    Sophie (Fr.); Sophia, Sophy
Sofronia (Gk.) wise
    Sophronia
Solada (Thai) listener
Solange (Fr.) solemn, dignified
Soledad (Sp.) solitary
    Sole, Chole
Solenne (Fr.) solemn, dignified; var. Solange
    Soline, Solène, Solaine, Souline, Solana, Solenna,
    Solen, Silana, Zéline, Solonez
Soloma (Heb.) peace
Solva (Nord.) healing warrior
Solveig (Nord.) healing drink; (L) solemn; (Teut.) sun
    power
    Solvig, Solvey, Solveiga
Sonia (Gk.) wisdom
    Sonya (Slav.)
Sophie (Fr., Gk.) wisdom
    Sophia, Sofia, Sophy, Sofie, Sonja, Sonya, Sonia,
    Soffi, Zofia, Sofija, Zoffi, Fia
Sophora (Fr.) flower name
Soraya (Persian) ancient princess, former queen of
    Iran; (Arab.) precious stone
Sorcha (Celt.) bright
Sosana (Heb.) lily
Souline (Fr.) solemn; var. Solange, Solenne
Soumitra (Hindi) wife of King Dasharatha, father of
    Lord Rama, incarnation of God
Souzan (Persian) firelike
Speranza (It.) hope
Sperata (It.) hoped for
    Esperanza (Sp.); Espérance (Fr.)
Stacie (Gk.) resurrection; var. Anastasia
    Stacy, Stacia, Tacey
Stacy (Gk., Irish) resurrection; (L) stable
Stanca (Slav. from L) firm

Star (L) star
   Starr
Stella (L) star
   Estelle (Fr.), Estela (It., Sp.); Estrella, Estrellita
   (Sp.); Steile, Stella, Essie
Stella-Maris (Sp. from L) star of the sea
Stephanie (Gk.) crown; fem. Stephen
   Stéphane, Stéphanie, Etiennette (Fr.); Stephana,
   Stefana, Stephania, Stefania, Stepanida
Suchin (Thai) beautiful thought
Sue (Heb.) lily; dim. Susan
Sueva—var. Susan
Sugi (Japanese) cedar
Suhaila (Arab.) star
Suké (Japanese) beloved
Sulaga (Arab.) last drops in the cup
Sulamita (Sp. from Heb.) complete, perfect
Sulia (L) downy, youthful
   Suliana
Sumalee (Thai) beautiful flower
Sumi (Japanese) refined
Suna (Japanese) sand; (Turk.) cypress, pheasant
   Soonah (Turk.)
Sunee (Thai) good thing
Sunita (Hindi) good conduct and deeds
Supriya (Hindi) greatly loved
Suruchi (Hindi) one who has nice ways
Susan (Heb.) lily
   Susana, Susanna (It., Sp.); Suzanne (Fr.); Suzan-
   nah, Suzette, Suzel, Suzy, Sosanna, Susie, Sue,
   Suki, Sussi, Zuzanna, Zsa Zsa, Siusan, Shusha,
   Shoshanna
Suté (Japanese) foresaken, foundling
Suzu (Japanese) little bell
Suzuë (Japanese) branch of little bells
Svetlana (Russ.) star, bright, shiny
Swana (Teut.) swan
   Swann

Swanhilda (Teut.) swan girl
Sylphide (Fr.) var. Sylvie
Sylvanna (L) forest
    Sylvaine, Sylvia, Silva, Silvia, Silvanna, Sylvette,
    Sylviane (Fr.)
Sylvie (Fr.) Sylvia

T

Tabby (Aramaic) gazelle
    Tabita, Tabitha, Taberia (Ger.)
Tadewi (Omaha Indian) wind woman
Taffy (Welsh from Heb.) beloved
    Tafline
Tahani (Arab.) congratulations
Tahira (Arab.) pure
Tahsin (Arab.) good deed
Taigi (Omaha Indian) returning new moon
Taini (Omaha Indian) coming new moon
Tainn (Ponca Indian) new moon
Taka (Japanese) honor, lofty
Takara (Japanese) treasure
Také (Japanese) bamboo
Taki (Japanese) waterfall
Tala (Persian) gold
Taliba (Arab.) student
Talitha (Aramaic) damsel arise
Tallia (L) third; (Gk.) abundance
    Talya
Talutah (Sioux Indian) scarlet, brilliant
Tama (Japanese) jewel
Tamaë (Japanese) jewel branch
Tamaki (Japanese) ring, bracelet
Tamara (Heb., Russ.) palm tree

Tamarah, Tammara, Tamar, Thamar, Tammy,
Tammie
Tamarat (Arab.) fruit
Tamasine—fem. Thomas
Tamassa, Tammy
Tamé (Japanese) for the sake of, unselfish
Tamora—Shakespearean character, queen of the
Goths
Tané (Japanese) seed
Tani (Japanese) valley
Tania (Slav.) fairy queen; dim. Tatiana
Tanya
Taqiya (Arab.) fear God
Tara (Celt.) tower, Irish king's residence
Taraneh (Persian) melody
Taru (Japanese) cask, barrel
Tasanee (Thai) beautiful view
Taslim (Arab.) peace
Tate (A-S) cheerful
Tayte, Taite
Tatiana (Russ.) fairy queen; (L) king of Sabines
Tanya, Tania, Tana, Tanaïs, Tyana, Tatienne (Fr.)
Tayaba (Arab.) pleasant
Tayanita (Cherokee Indian) young beaver
Tayce (Fr.) silence
Tace, Tacey
Tazu (Japanese) ricefield stork
Tecla (Ger., It.) divine fame
Thecle, Thecla
Tegene (Ethiopian) my support
Tehya (American Indian) precious
Teïla (Celt., Gk.) people
Tella
Temperance (L) temperance
Temple (L) temple
Templa
Teofila (It.) divinely loved
Terah (Heb.) flourishing
Terentilla (L) tender

Terenzia—fem. Terence
    Terry, Terencia, Terentia, Terentine, Teriokha, Tiocha, Teria, Terris, Terentille
Teresa (Gk., It., Sp.) harvester; (Heb.) beautiful
    Theresa, Teressa, Thérèse (Fr.); Terza, Tessa, Tess, Tessie, Terka, Tesja, Tracy, Resa, Resi, Resia
Terra (L) earth
Terry—short Teresa, Terenzia
    Terrie
Tertia (L) third
    Terza
Tesceline (Fr.) fem. var. Anselm, Asceline
Tessa (Gk.) fourth; short Teresa
Tessema (Ethiopian) to be listened to
Tetsu (Japanese) iron
Thadine (Heb.) praised; fem. dim. Thaddeus
Thaïs (Fr., Gk.) bond, lovely
Thalassa (Gk.) sea
Thalia (Gk.) bloom, muse of comedy
    Thalie
Thaw (Burmese) noisy
Thea (Gk.) divine
    Theïa
Thecla (Gk.) divine fame
    Thekla
Thelma (Gk.) nursling
Themis (Gk.) goddess of law and justice
Theodora (Gk.) divine gift
    Theda, Theodosia, Feodora (Russ.); Teodora (It.); Fiodora, Dora, Fedorka, Didi, Fedia, Dorsie, Fediana, Fedoulia, Diounia, Dioussia, Fedoussia
Theola (Gk.) divine
Theone (Gk.) godly
Theophania (Ger., Gk.) divine manifestation
    Theophanie (Fr.); Theophana
Theophila (Gk.) divinely loved
    Theofila, Teofilia (It.)

Thera (Gk.) wild
Thetis (Gk.) mythological figure, mother of Achilles; sea nymph
Thin (Burmese) learned
Thirza (Heb.) delight, pleasantness
Thisbe—Babylonian girl loved by Pyramus in legend
Thomasina (Heb.) twin; fem. Thomas
  Tomasina, Tomasine, Tomasa (It.)
Thora (Scand.) fem. Thor
Thya (Gk.) perfume
Tiana—dim. Tatiana
Tiara—flower name
Tibbie (Scot. from Heb.) God's oath
Tiberia (It.) of the Tiber
Tida (Thai) daughter
Tienette (Fr. from Gk.) crown; fem. dim. Stephen
Tiffany—short Theophania
  Tiffanie, Tiphaine, Tiphanie (Fr.)
Tilda (Teut.) heroine; short Mathilda
  Tilly, Tillie
Timandra (Gk.) honor, Shakespearean character
  Tymandra, Tima
Timothea (Gk.) honors God
Tina—short Christina, Martina et al.
Tirza (Sp. from Heb.) cypress
Toby (Heb.) good
Toinette (Fr. from L) beyond praise; short Antoinette
  Tonneli (Swiss); Tonia (It., Sp.) Toni, Tonette
Tolla (L) victor
Tomi (Japanese) riches
Tomiju (Japanese) wealth and longevity
Tonia—short Antonia
Topaz—precious stone
Tora (Japanese) tiger; var. Thora
  Torina, Thorina, Tura
Torli (Swiss from Gk.) gift of God
Tory—short Victoria
Toshi (Japanese) arrowhead

Tote (Basque) ancient Visigoth name
Tovi (Heb., Swiss) beloved
Toveli
Tracy (Gk.) harvester; (A-S) brave; short Anastasia,
Teresa et al.
Trella (Sp.) star; short Estrella
Trenel (Gk.) pure
Trili, Trine (Swiss); Tryn (Dut.); Trind (Scand.);
Trinette (Fr.)
Tressa—var. Teresa
Trina—dim. Catrina
Trinette
Trista—fem. Tristan
Tristana, Trestana
Troya (Gk.) Trojan
Trojane, Troia, Troyenne, Troy
Trude—short Gertrude
Trudie, Trudel
Tsuhgi (Japanese) next, second child
Tsuna (Japanese) bond
Tsuné (Japanese) constance
Tsuru (Japanese) stork, longevity
Tula—var. Gertrude
Tullia (L) third
Tullie, Tuliane
Turaya (Arab.) star
Tyana—var. Tatiana

U

Udele (A-S) rich
Ufuk (Turk.) sunset
Ula (Celt.) jewel of the sea; (Basque) name for Virgin
    Mary
    Uli
Ulla (Ger., Scand.) will; var. Ulrica
Ulrika (Ger., Russ.) fem. Ulric
    Ulrica, Ulrike, Ulla, Rika, Rica, Uli
Umay (Turk.) hope
Umé (Japanese) plum blossom
Umégaë (Japanese) plum-tree spray
Uméno (Japanese) plum-tree field
Una (L) one
Undine (Ger. from L) waves
    Ondine
Unna (Teut.) woman
Urania (Gk.) heavenly
    Uranie (Fr.); Ourania, Ouranie
Urano (Japanese) coast; short, field
Urbana (Sp.) of the town
    Urbaine, Urbane (Fr.), Urbanilla
Urika (Omaha Indian) useful to all
Ursa (L) bear
    Ursel, Ursule (Fr.); Ursula (Ger., Russ.); Ursilla,
    Ursillane, Ursina, Orsola, Orsolya, Oursa
Ursula (L) bear
    Ursuline, Ursulina, Ursela, Ursel
Uta (Ger.) rich; (Japanese) poem, song
    Utako (Japanese)
Utano (Japanese) song field

V

Val—short Valentine, Valerie
    Valya (Russ.)
Valda (Teut.) fem. Valdis, Valdemar; (Sp.) heroine
Valeda (L) strong
Valencia (L) strong
Valentine (L) strong, brave
    Valentina (It., Russ., Sp.); Valentiane, Vallie,
    Valeda, Valida, Valentyn, Valensia, Lalensia, Val-
    latina, Valiaka
Valerie (L) strong
    Valery, Valeria, Valya, Valia, Valeska, Valyush-
    ka, Valeriana
Valonia (L) of the valley
Vanessa (Gk.) butterfly
    Vanesa, Vania, Vanny, Vanna
Vania (Heb.) God's gracious gift
    Vanina
Vanida (Thai) girl
Vara (Gk.) stranger; (Slav.) dim. Barbara
    Varinka (Russ.)
Varaporn (Thai) angel's clothing
Varda (Heb.) rose
    Vadit
Variana (L) varied
Varouna—Indian mythological goddess of the waters
Vashti (Persian) beautiful
Veda (Sanskrit) knowledge
Vedette (Fr.) watchtower
Vega (Scand. from L) star
Veia—fem. Hervé
    Veïane, Veig

Vela (L) wish
    Vella
Velda (Dut.) field
    Velida, Valida
Veleda (Teut.) wise woman
Velia (Sp.) pre-Roman place name; (OGer.) happy;
    var. Evelia
Velika (Russ.) great
Velinda—var. Belinda
Vellore (Hindi) name of town
Velma—var. Vilma; pet Wilhelmina
Veneta (L) of Venice
    Venita
Venetia (Celt.) blessed
    Venice
Ventura (It. from L) well met, happy
Venus (L) goddess of love and beauty in Greek and
    Roman mythology
Vera (L) truth; (Russ.) faith
    Vérane, Vérania, Vérèna, Véréne, Vérenne, Vir-
    iane (Fr.); Viera, Veradis, Varena, Verana, Ver-
    ania, Veranina, Vren, Vreni, Vrenele, Verushka
Verda (It., Sp. from L) fresh
Verdad (Sp.) truth
Vere (Fr.) from Ver in Normandy; var. Vera
Vered (Heb.) rose
Verena (OGer.) fem. Warren; var. Vera
    Verina
Veridienne (Fr.) greenery
Verita (L) truth
    Verity
Verna (L) truth, springtime
    Verne, Vernita
Veronica (L) truth, true image; var. Berenice
    Veronika (Ger.); Véronique (Fr.), Veronica (Sp.);
    Veronik, Veroushka (Slav.); Verounia, Beronika,
    Berenike
Vesma (L) vessel
    Vesna

Vespera (OFr.) star
Vesta (L) Roman goddess of fire, home
Veva (Celt.) white wave; short Genoveva
    Vevay
Vevina (Celt., Scot.) melodious woman
Victoria (L) victorious
    Victoire, Victorine, Victoriane (Fr.); Vittoria
    (It.); Vitoria (Sp.); Vicky, Vicki, Vitousha, Vic-
    torienne, Fieke, Vitiana, Gwthyr, Viktorina
Vida (Heb.) beloved; (Welsh) fem. David
Vidette (Heb.) beloved
Viena (OFr.) invite
Vilma—pet Wilhelmina
    Velma
Vilna—pet Wilhelmina
Vina (Sp.) divine; dim. Divina
Vinetia—var. Venetia
    Venita
Vinnette (Fr.) pet Winifred
Vinnulia (L) winning
Viola (L) violet
    Violeta, Violante (Sp.); Violetta (It.); Violet,
    Violette, Violaine, Viole (Fr.); Vila, Violka
    (Slav.); Lola, Letta, Ola, Olia, Vela, Vye, Vi
Virgile (L) flourishing
    Virgiliane (Fr.); Virgilise, Virgila,
    Virgilia, Virgiliz
Virginia (L) pure
    Virginie, Virgine, Virge (Fr.); Virguinia, Virginia
    (It.); Ginnie, Ginny, Ginger, Guinia
Viridiana (L) greenery
Viridis (L) green, youthful
Virna (L) truth
    Verna, Verena
Vitaliana (L) living
    Vita, Vida, Vitalina
Viveca (L, Scand.) living voice
Vivian (L) lively
    Vivien, Vivienne, Viviane, Vivia, Bibiane (Fr.);

Viviana (It., Sp.); Vivina, Bibiana (Sp.); Bibiñe (Basque); Vivine, Veïa, Vivianka, Vibienne, Vivi, Vyvyan, Viven

Voëlle (Celt., Fr.) view

Volante—var. Violette
Voletta

Voleta (OFr.) veiled

Vona—dim. Yvonne

W

Waala (Arab.) take refuge

Wagai (Ethiopian) my treasure, my prize

Wahida (Arab.) unique

Wajida (Arab.) excited

Wakana (Japanese) plant name

Walda (OE) forest; (OGer.) rule

Walida (Arab.) newborn girl

Wallis (OE) wall; (ONorse) choice
Wallice

Wanda (OE) young tree; (OGer.) ruler; (Ger.) marvelous
Wandis, Wandie, Wandala, Wandula, Wenda, Vanda, Wendy, Wendie, Wendeline

Wanjiru (Kikuyu, Kenya) one of nine tribes

Wasima (Arab.) pretty

Wenda (OE) fair
Wendeline, Wendy, Gwendaline

Wendela (Teut.) wandering
Wendeline

Wesla (OE) from west meadow

Whitney (A-S) white island

Wilda (OE) willow; (A-S) wild

Wil**en**—short Wilhelmina
elmina—fem. Wilhelm

Wilhelmine (Fr.); Vilma, Wilma, Minella, Helma, Willa, Wilmette, Elma, Minna, Minnie, Helmina, Gulielma, Guillelmina (It., Sp.); Willabelle, Vilna, Mimi, Minette

Willa (A-S) desired; short Wilhelmina
Wilone, Wilona

Winifred (Teut.) friend of peace; (Welsh) white wave; combination Winnie and Freda
Winnie, Winfrieda, Winefred, Winnifred, Wina

Winona (Sioux Indian) eldest daughter, charitable

X

Xanthe (Gk.) blonde
Xavière (Fr. from Basque) new house; fem. Xavier
Xaviera
Xenia (Gk., Russ.) hospitality
Zenia
Xylia (Gk.) wood
Xylina

Y

Yaa (Ashanti tribe, Ghana) Thursday's child
Yael (Heb.) ascent
Jael, Yalit
Yaella (Arab.) prominent
Yaffa (Heb.) beautiful
Yafit, Jaffa
Yakira (Heb.) valuable
Yanamari (Basque) combination Jean and Marie

Yanna (Heb.) God's grace
Yardena (Heb.) descendant
    Jordana
Yarkona (Heb.) green
Yasmeen (Persian) flower
    Yasmina, Yasmine, Jasime, Jasmin, Jasmina, Jessamyn
Yasu (Japanese) tranquil
Yatra (Heb.) good
Yedida (Heb.) friend
Yehiela (Heb.) may God live
    Jehiela
Yehudit (Heb.) praise
    Yuta, Judith, Judit, Judinta
Yeira (Heb.) light
Yemina (Heb.) right hand
Yera (Basque) name for Virgin Mary
Yeshisha (Heb.) old
Yetta—pet Henrietta
    Yitta
Yigal (Heb.) redeem
Yma (Heb.) mother
    Ima, Imma
Yo (Japanese) positive
    Yoko, dim.
Yoanna—var. Joanna
Yocheved (Heb.) God is glorious
    Yochebed
Yolande (OFr.) violet; (OGer.) country
    Yolanda (Sp.); Violante, Viola, Yolante, Yola, Iole, Yolenta, Iolana, Yoléne, Jolanda, Jola, Eolande, Jolanthe
Yôn (Burmese) rabbit
Yona (Heb.) dove
    Yonah, Yonina, Yonita
Yoné (Japanese) wealth (literally, rice)
       (Coos Indian) star
    panese) trustworthy
    apanese) good

Yoshino (Japanese) good, fertile field
Yovela (Heb.) rejoicing
Ysabel—var. Isabelle
Yseulte (Celt.) fair; heroine legend of Tristan and
    Yseult
    Isolde, Ysolt
Ysole (Fr. from OGer.) ice
    Ysoline
Yu-jun (Chinese) from Chongching
Yulene (Basque) fem. Jordan
Yuri (Japanese) lily
    Yuriko, dim.
Yvette (Fr.) fem. Yves.
Yvon (Irish) fem. Ives
Yvonne (Fr. from Scand.) archer; fem. Yves
    Yvon, Yveline, Ivona, Vonne, Vonnie, Ivetta, Iva,
    Yvonnick, Yvona, Ivonne, Nonna

Z

Zabrina—var. Sabrina
Zafina (Arab.) victorious
Zahida (Arab.) ascetic
Zahira (Arab.) outstanding, luminous
Zahra (Arab.) blossom
Zaida (Arab.) growing
Zaira (Arab.) flowery
Zakia (Heb.) bright, pure
    Zakit
Zakira (Arab.) remembrance
Zakyia (Arab.) pure
Zandra—var. Sandra
Zaneta (Heb.) God's gracious gift
Zara (Arab.) brightness of the East; (Heb.) dawn; var.
    Sarah

Zarifa (Arab.) graceful
Zariza (Heb.) industrious
    Zeriza
Zayit (Heb.) olive
    Zetta
Zayn (Arab.) graceful
Zea—var. Zoe
Zedena (L) of Sidon
Zeena—flower name
    Zina, Ninnia
Zehava (Heb.) golden
    Zahava, Zehuva, Zehavit, Zehavi
Zehira (Heb.) guarded
Zela—var. Zoe
Zelda (OE) rare; short Griselda
    Selda
Zelia (L) zealous
    Zella, Zeline, Zelie
Zena (Ethiopian) news; (Persian) woman
    Zenana (Persian)
Zenaida (Gk., Russ.) daughter of Zeus
    Zenaide (Fr.); Zina, Zena
Zenda (Persian) sacred, womanly
Zenebe (Ethiopian) rained
Zenevieva (Celt., Russ.) white wave; var. Genevieve,
    Geneva
    Zinerva
Zenia (Gk.) hospitable
Zenobia (Arab.) father's ornament; (Gk.) stranger,
    symbol
    Zenovia (Russ.); Zena; Zinaida (Gr.)
Zenodora (Gk.) stranger
Zeona (Heb.) sign
    Ziona
Zephaniah (Heb.) protected of the Lord, Jah is hidden
Zephira (Heb.) morning
Zephyr (Gk.) west wind
Zephyrine (Fr., Gk.) like the zephyr
Zerah (Heb.) rising of light

Zerelda (Teut.) armored
  Serilda
Zerlina—heroine in Mozart's *Don Giovanni*
Zerom (Ethiopian) their seed
Zerren (Turk.) narcissus
Zerrin (Turk.) golden
Zeynep (Turk.) ornament
Zezili (Basque) Cecile
Zila (Heb.) shadow, shade
  Zilla, Hillah
Zilpha (Heb.) sprinkling
  Zylpha
Zimra (Heb.) branch, song of praise
  Zimria, Zemira, Zemora, Zamora
Zippora (Heb.) bird
  Sippora
Zira (Heb.) arena
Zita (Arab.) mistress; dim. Teresa
Zitkala (Dakota Indian) bird
Ziva (Heb.) brightness
  Zivit
Zoara (Arab.) mythological goddess of love
Zoe (Gk.) life
  Zoë, Zoa, Zoey, Zoé, Zoelie, Zoelle (Fr.)
Zohar (Arab., Heb.) brilliance
Zoheret (Heb.) she shines
Zohreh (Persian) happiness; (Arab.) flower
  Zora
Zoia (Gk., Russ.) life
  Zoya
Zonta (Sioux Indian) trustworthy
Zonya—var. Sonia
  Zonia
Zora (Slav.) dawn; var. Sara
  Zorana, Zoreen, Zorna
Zoraida (Arab.) eloquent
Zozima (Gk.) vigorous
Zubayda (Arab.) best part
Zudora (Sanskrit) laborer

Zuelia (Arab.) peace
    Zulema, Zuleika
Zuharat (Arab.) flower
Zuleika (Arab.) brilliant, beautiful
    Zeleeka
Zulema (Arab.) healthy, vigorous
    Zulima
Zuria (Basque) Blanche

THE FINEST CHILD CARE
TITLES FROM POCKET BOOKS

☐ **DR. SPOCK'S BABY AND CHILD CARE**
Benjamin Spock, M.D. and Michael B. Rothenberg, M.D.
69529-0/$6.99

☐ **HOW TO RAISE A BRIGHTER CHILD**
Joan Beck..........73999-9/$5.50

☐ **THE MAGIC OF ENCOURAGEMENT**
Stephanie Marston.........73273-0/$9.00

☐ **THE MIRACLE YEAR**
Lanie Carter with Lauren Simon Ostrow
70432-X/$8.00

☐ **THE NEW MOTHER SYNDROME**
Carol Dix.......................64485-8/$4.50

☐ **THE PARENTING CHALLENGE**
Arnold Rincover, Ph.D. ....68163-X/$9.00

☐ **RAISING YOUR TYPE A CHILD**
Dr. Steven Shelov and John Kelly
69244-5/$9.00

☐ **79 WAYS TO CALM A CRYING BABY**
Diana S. Greene...........66247-3/$6.00

POCKET BOOKS

Simon & Schuster Mail Order
200 Old Tappan Rd., Old Tappan, N.J. 07675

Please send me the books I have checked above. I am enclosing $_____ (please add $0.75 to cover the postage and handling for each order. Please add appropriate sales tax). Send check or money order—no cash or C.O.D.'s please. Allow up to six weeks for delivery. For purchase over $10.00 you may use VISA: card number, expiration date and customer signature must be included.

Name _____

Address _____

City _____ State/Zip _____

VISA Card # _____ Exp.Date _____

Signature _____ 700

Having Your Baby...
Raising Your Child

_____ 72760-5 **BABY NAMES FROM AROUND THE WORLD**
Maxine Fields $4.99

_____ 76060-2 **DR. SPOCK'S BABY AND CHILD CARE**
Benjamin Spock, M.D. and
Michael Rothenberg M.D. $6.99

_____ 70962-3 **WHAT SHALL WE NAME THE BABY?**
Ed. Winthrop Ames $4.50

_____ 73901-8 **BOY OR GIRL?**
Dr. Elizabeth Whelan $5.50

_____ 74548-4 **NURSING YOUR BABY**
Karen Pryor $5.95

_____ 69380-8 **TOILET TRAINING IN LESS THAN A DAY**
Dr. Nathan Azri
& Dr. Richard M. Foxx $4.50

FULLY REVISED AND UPDATED FOR THE 1990s

The one essential parenting book that has been the century's greatest bestseller is now fully updated for the next generation of parents and children and the challenging world of the 1990s.

DR. SPOCK'S BABY AND CHILD CARE

BENJAMIN SPOCK, M.D., and MICHAEL B. ROTHENBERG, M.D.

Available from Pocket Books

POCKET
B O O K S